How
to Be
the Best
Candidate
Every
Single
Time

How to Be the Best Candidate Every Single Time

A recruitment guide by
Heather Watt, MSc FCIPD

FUZZY FLAMINGO

First published in 2025 by Fuzzy Flamingo
Copyright © Heather Watt 2025

Heather Watt has asserted her right to be identified as the author of this Work in accordance with the Copyright, Designs and Patents Act 1988.

ISBN: 978-1-0684468-4-9

Editing and design by Fuzzy Flamingo
www.fuzzyflamingo.co.uk

A catalogue for this book is available from the British Library.

This book is dedicated to my husband, Brian. He's my best friend and biggest fan, although his CV is still seven pages long. Some people need to do things their own way.

Where will you begin?

What are your priorities right now?

You can find out more about me by visiting my website (https://www.heatherwatt.
co.uk/) and reading my blog (https://www.heatherwatt.co.uk/tea-break).

Just saying hello ...

I've written this guide to help you survive and conquer the modern UK jobs market. Recruitment can feel like a merry-go-round (spinning out of control) or a maze (confused, lost). Everyone seems to know something about recruitment, although few are prepared to master its complexity and often declare that recruitment is broken!

Employers often create recruitment policy and processes without much care for the people they hope to attract and secure to join them. Whether you're conceptual or detailed, creative or analytical, there's something in this guide for you. It's packed with variety, fun and opportunity.

I hope you agree the guide is written in an easy and engaging style that appeals to a broad spectrum of people seeking work, whatever their current experience levels. For me, there are some basic principles that job seekers can master to increase their chances of success. The principles remain constant across different business sectors and professional groups, as well as organisational levels or experience.

Standing out in a crowd for all the right reasons is the priority. Many organisations modify their recruitment processes according to job type or job level, although I don't see any need to create a different text for students seeking their first job or executives hoping to join the board.

I've created a guide, which is written for you and your ambitions if you're:

- Wishing to break into the jobs market for the first time
- Needing to better understand the modern UK jobs market
- Seeking a career or job change
- Wanting to fight off feelings of negativity following redundancy
- Feeling demoralised by recruitment experiences

Whether you're a person who likes the detail or someone who prefers to skim the text and get stuck into the tasks, there's something in this guide for you. And you don't even need to approach it in the same order as everyone else.

Fundamental to your success is knowing yourself and what you want to achieve from your work. That's why I've created some written tasks to help you define your strengths and achievements and tell your story. Writing everything down will help you to remember where it all began.

If you haven't got time for that right now, I recommend beginning with the chapter or section that's most likely to help with your current challenges. When you've more time, you can tackle the earlier chapters. For example, if you've got an interview in a few days, it's time to prepare and practise. A new CV can come later.

About me

"Success isn't about how much money you make.
It's about the difference you make in people's lives."

Michelle Obama, September 2012

I wanted to share a few insights with you, so that you know who you are dealing with before we get started on working together. After all, you'll be sharing some of your work secrets and ambitions with me. That's why I've included one of my favourite quotes, which sums up how I like to work.

From time to time, I've thought about writing a business text on recruitment. I've even rehearsed some of the chapters in my head. Every so often, some of the ideas I've been cultivating spill over into my blog (https://www.heatherwatt.co.uk/tea-break) alongside favourite recipes and gardening tips. Feedback has been positive, although right now, I've swapped any notion of academic commentary for a more inspirational approach to helping you with your job search.

I've been writing for my blog since March 2019, and I'm pleased that my reflections have connected with so many people. It's the things that I do and the people I meet who inspire me. My zest for life, interest in recruitment trends and search for HR excellence all influence what I do and how I work. I love the garden, and have a passion for baking, although right now, my vision is to create a guide that will support job seekers like you. A guide that's all about shared experience and strategies to help you succeed.

The business edit

I am an independent consultant, coach and writer with a reputation for delivering success. I share my creativity, extensive HR experience and specialist knowledge (resourcing expertise) with individuals and organisations to make their aspirations a reality and to inspire learning.

An influential communicator and passionate collaborator, I partner with individuals, as well as local and global businesses to get things done. Noted for innovation, creativity and transformation, I measure my success in terms of shared expertise, performance improvements and lasting partnerships.

My reputation

A friend once described me as: "The person people want to talk to at a bus stop or in the baker's queue." I didn't deny it, it's so true, although I don't set out to interview everyone I meet – I'm simply good at asking questions.

I'm curious, innovative and creative. I love my garden and baking, although trust me, over the years, I've tried so many different upcycling ideas and even selling vintage clothes. More recently, I've taken up writing and Indian block printing, but that's another story for another day.

My HR career began more years ago than I'm going to let on here, although if you know me already, you'll have some idea. Early aspirations to design furniture soon took a back seat when I recognised my interest in the people who make a business successful.

A dedicated networker, I enjoy bringing people together to share experience and knowledge. I love what I do at work; it's all about collaboration and conversation – I do both well. If something needs to change or you need a fresh approach, beginning the conversation is the most difficult thing you'll need to do. And I'm here to help you with that conversation.

The idea for this guide grew from a set of recruitment principles and related guidance I developed during lockdowns. The guide is packed with helpful advice, creative ideas for you to try and lots of positivity – it's what I do well. I haven't included any recipes or horticultural tips here (they're reserved for my blog), although I hope to keep you interested.

My credentials

I've been creating recruitment processes and resourcing strategies for decades. Designing HR learning materials and delivering interview skills workshops became a passion in the early nineties and I haven't looked back. I'm proud to be a recruitment trailblazer. I'm proud of my knowledge and my skills, although it's my personality that brings it all together. Personality is like adding a twist of lime to your drink to make it come alive.

I'm up for helping you to find your twist of lime (your zing) and create your story. I can help you stand out from the crowd for all the right reasons by telling your story in the most engaging way. And I can help you to better understand what you need from your work and how your superpowers can help you with your ambitions. **Are you ready?**

This is your gig, not mine!

I can help you:
- Get to know yourself, your strengths and your ambitions a little better
- Create and upload a sparkling CV with a genius covering letter
- Follow the instructions provided to create a brilliant presentation
- Answer interview questions with style and confidence
- Evaluate offers and make the right choices for you

About recruitment

There's already a whole heap of recruitment advice available (much of it readily accessible online) and most people you meet will have an opinion on how to use it. So, why is it still so difficult to feel like you've got it right? Spoiler alert: maybe it's because it doesn't really help you to move forward or to inspire you to change. That's how this guide is different. It's written to encourage you to:

- Try out innovative ideas
- Work in a new way and
- Thrive

Most people I meet have a recruitment story they want to share and an opinion they hope I'll validate, although how many of us have had a good recruitment experience? Employers need people to collaborate with them and (most) people want to work, so how and why did the matching process create so much negativity and complexity?

My simple definition begins with a job advert (or agent's call) and candidate applications ahead of candidate interviews and a job offer to one lucky candidate. So many people seem to know best how to do it, yet few do it well – just like scoring goals in football.

Defining recruitment
· Begins with an advert or a call from an agent or headhunter then your application
· Almost always includes an interview or several interviews (and other tasks)
· Diverse interview types – biographical, competency-based, scenario-based
· Additional elements – questionnaires about your work preferences, tests, case studies
· Designed to understand how you work and think
· Your opportunity to shine

There are probably as many different application or selection processes as there are stars in the sky and, like stars, some you can see and some you can't. The variations are infinite. If you are an actor, a musician or a dancer, then your process is likely to include an audition. Similarly, designers may be asked to deliver a creative task, retailers their business plans or fashionistas their seasonal predictions. That's why I've summarised the popular activities and assessments you may come across, along with my best advice for your success.

So, just to be clear, I'm keeping my recruitment advice and messaging simple: if you do *this*, it's likely *this* will be the outcome. I've included some background to support my proposals and some alternatives you might prefer. You won't find me telling you what to do without explanation. My goal is to simplify the jargon associated with recruitment.

The current jobs market is tough and it's not going to be a leisurely ride for you, although I plan to make it enjoyable for both of us. **Are you up for the challenge?**

About you

Unless you're looking for your first job, it's likely that you're reading this because you know that you need to find a new opportunity to inspire you and it's time for a change. Perhaps you've simply had enough of what work throws at you, or you're unemployed already. Maybe you were at the top of your game in what has become a particularly tough sector like hospitality or high street retail and now feel a little unloved. Whether you're a leader or a follower, an entrepreneur or an aviator, there's always benefit in understanding yourself better.

Sometimes it's good to go back to the basics of what you're about – your strengths and achievements all contribute to your story. Think of it as a way of establishing your credentials. A great benefit if you're needing to make a name for yourself in a fresh context. For example, cabin crew to customer service manager, chief operating officer (COO) to chief executive (CEO).

If you're up for the challenge, why not give it a go? Chapter One will help to guide you through this tried and tested technique I use with individual clients. I get to ask questions to keep our conversation on track. You may find it helpful to work through the chapter with a friend or someone from your network, although it works just as well without collaboration. **Have fun!**

A blank sheet of paper

Sometimes we underestimate our capabilities because we get a bit stuck in the weeds of what didn't go so well and self-doubt creeps in. That's the time to dig deep and remember what you've learned from other activities like recycling or selling your unwanted stuff, family budgeting and organising events as a volunteer.

Once the Chapter One tasks are complete, you'll have an up-to-date view of your strengths and achievements, which you can explore further in Chapter Two to refresh your unique story. You can always press the pause button if it doesn't seem to be helping – nobody's judging you, and I won't be offended. I'm just encouraging you to continue with a clear head.

Benefits of decluttering

Now you've re-established your credentials, it'll be so much easier to declutter your CV and your online presence. All this should help with your storytelling and how you answer interview questions. Here's hoping that you enjoy updating what you know about yourself. **There's so much in this guide to help you.**

Remember that this guide is written for you if you're:

- Wishing to break into the jobs market for the first time
- Needing to better understand the modern UK jobs market
- Seeking a career or job change
- Wanting to fight off feelings of negativity following redundancy
- Feeling demoralised by recruitment experiences

About this guide

Congratulations, you've taken the plunge and invested in this guide to help you. Now it's up to me to help you to make the investment work for you. It's packed full of advice, helpful information and tips as well as some learning tasks for you to try. I've included some worked examples to help you get through the tasks just in case you need them.

But that doesn't let you off the hook! Securing a new role (whether that's part-time, full-time or a 'side hustle') takes commitment, courage and time. It's not easy,[i] although with some help from your friends and your networks, it can be so much more enjoyable. With this guide to hand in all its glory, I hope that you'll have some fun along the way. **Let's learn together!**

Learning tasks[ii]	Top tips

My audience

Controversial always, shy never, I've created this guide for as broad and diverse an audience as I could imagine. I'm not a fan of different messages for different professionals or organisational levels. I've no desire to exclude recent college leavers or promote

---

i   Chapter Fourteen highlights some of the challenges.

ii   To make the investment work for you, this book is packed full of advice, helpful information and tips, as well as some learning tasks for you to try. I've included some worked examples to help you get through the tasks just in case you need them.

unnecessarily complex strategies for business leaders or entrepreneurs. That said, I accept that one size doesn't *always* fit all and I'll leave it up to you how you make use of the concepts and their underlying principles to suit your needs.

Your superstar qualities

I've written this guide to help you to explore possibilities and stay positive. Being the best candidate means understanding yourself and what you offer potential employers. I can't promise you a new role immediately, although I can help you to better understand your superpowers. With this guide, I'm here to help you create your story and tell it in the most engaging way – whether that's a newly designed CV, on your socials or at interview.

Your story

It's important that we get our recruitment conversations off to a strong and positive start, so this guide begins with a chapter on knowing (or finding) your strengths and what's important to you at work. I'll help you pinpoint what you like to do and how you like to do it. You may be desperate to secure a new role and eager to get to the chapter on creating a fabulous CV, but first we need to understand what you're bringing to the party.

In a hurry

You can use this guide to gain insight to a particular recruitment challenge or fix a problem as it crops up. If you don't have time or the inclination to begin with Chapter One outlined above, I've included a route map to help you find your way around the chapters. Once you're hooked on my innovative ideas and how they can help you, I hope that you'll work through Chapters One and Two before going on to tackle the chapters on creating sparkling CVs and preparing for interview.

Practise makes perfect

From time to time, I've provided you with opportunities to record your ideas and progress. You get to decide what works best for you, although try to commit to words on a page, rather than vague concepts in your head (it's good to practise aloud). That's why I recommend writing directly into this guide or keeping an electronic journal. Love 'em or loathe 'em, these written activities and learning tasks can be fun to look back on when reviewing your progress.

Controversial or simply different

At the end of some sections, I include alternative options for you to consider, as well as the occasional super-controversial idea to get you noticed for all the right reasons. Super-controversial may not seem like your thing right now, and I know that a video CV isn't for everyone, but with a great big dollop of new-found confidence, who knows where your story will take you? This guide really is a box of tricks to be executed with style.

Getting noticed

Some of the topics and principles we'll explore together are not limited to recruitment. We're also going to practise some positive conversation techniques to take your communication skills to another level. A fabulous CV can be a great tool for getting noticed as a speaker, a panellist, podcaster or presenter, and even the next in line for promotion. Who knows how popular you'll be with your network once you've polished your story and can tell it with renewed confidence? Yes, this is your time to shine!

Learn as you go

I've created this guide with a focus on self-reflection and learning, rather than simply telling you what (or what not) to do. If you don't know the principle (the magic) behind the ideas, how can you make strong choices and apply your own unique brand of judgement to career decisions? It's time to experience change – read on to find out how.

Give it a try

Once you've tried a new way of doing something, it's helpful to consider how it went – what worked well (or not so well) – then think about what you need to change before trying it again. Now consider what you learned. Recognising where you could have done something differently or better will contribute to your personal development and overall strengths portfolio. Remember to focus on the positives and try not to beat yourself up when things don't go so well. There's a recruitment-related example to help you below.

Example

"
- **Plan** *your approach to answering interview questions – assemble some strong examples*
- **Use** *the strong examples at your next interview*
- **Review** *the impact of your examples – your initial reaction and any feedback received*
- **Revise** *or modify your approach and* **edit** *your answers in the light of your performance / any feedback received*
"

Jargon busting

Without wishing to offend all the talent acquisition directors I know, I've kept to the term recruitment throughout this guide (rather than talent acquisition or resourcing). My reasons, though valid, are irrelevant to this guide.

To increase readability, I've adopted the names 'headhunter' and 'recruiter', rather than search or recruitment consultant, or any other variations. And finally, I've used the term recruiter to mean any third-party agent or in-house professional engaged in the recruitment process, irrespective of their organisational level or title. Apologies in advance to anyone who's offended.

You'll find some further explanations and definitions on page 96 onwards. I've tried to avoid all but essential recruitment-related jargon in this guide, although sometimes it's worth knowing the full vocabulary. Additional knowledge may just increase your self-confidence when it's needed most. After all, knowledge is power sometimes, right?

Feedback

If you enjoy reading this guide and trying out new ways of doing things, then please recommend it to a friend or a colleague. And if it falls short in your view, please let me know. There's always room for improvement and I'm no prima donna – feedback helps me to improve what I offer. Are you ready to make a difference? **Let's do this!**

Top tip – Recording your progress by writing things down often helps you to see how far you've come and what you've changed.

Contents

A more traditional index for those who prefer this approach

A guided tour of what you've bought into

1. Know your strengths & achievements	2. Own your own story & tell it confidently	3. Create a sparkling CV – go on, I dare you!
Knowing what you're all about and what you offer employers – your strengths	Using storytelling to get your ideas and expectations across to your audience	Making sure your CV sparkles. Optimum layouts. Hints and tips for success
What you have to say to your audience – your achievements	Linking your learning with work experience and your aspirations for future success	Refreshing your CV. Writing up your achievements and your strengths, i.e. your story
Matching your values to employer values – what's important to you?	Keeping your communication on track, consistent and persuasive – CV to interview and beyond	Creating your first ever CV and where to begin. Balancing facts and examples
4. Understand your flexibility	**5. Stay in touch with your networks**	**6. Study your jobs market**
Being clear about how flexible you can be – working hours, location and reward	Understanding the benefits of networking and sharing job search experiences	Understanding what's happening in organisations or sectors of interest
Knowing your boundaries. What's essential and what's negotiable?	Staying connected to the people who might be able to help you with introductions	Keeping up to date with the growth sectors that are relevant to your expertise
Being realistic about what's achievable and practical, viz., study or work commitments	Sharing knowledge and ideas about job seeking and working with your network	Researching organisations that are of interest and recruiting consistently

7. Pursue jobs of interest	8. Tailor your communication	9. Research employers
Getting a focus on the opportunities that interest you and ignoring the rest	Composing applications, cover letters and emails that meet the brief	Recognising what you need to know about potential employers
Creating a plan to identify which jobs are most likely to interest you and why	Knowing when to tinker with your CV as requested by agents and when not to!	Knowing who can help you find out what you need to know about a role / business
Knowing it's okay to only invest time and effort in the jobs which interest you	Recognising the value of what you say, how you say it and how the audience reacts	Hanging on in there until you find out if an opportunity might work for you
10. Prepare for interviews & other assessments	11. Practise out loud	12. Be clear on your questions
Preparing for interviews, auditions, presentations and assessment centres, etc.	Realising the benefits of practising (your interview performance) aloud	Knowing which questions you want to ask potential employers or their agents
Getting an idea of what to expect from distinct types of recruitment events / interviews	Finding effective strategies to deliver the answers and ideas in your head	Making questions an essential part of your interview preparation
Answering questions with ease / confidence because you've structured content well	Making answers flow more freely because you've rehearsed in advance	Staying positive when it's time for your questions and your mind goes blank
13. Accept a role & flourish	14. It's not an easy ride	15. Our adventure together
Getting to know where you are most likely to flourish and what you'll be doing	Remembering to ask for help before you need it	Laying the foundations of your success
Comparing opportunities and deciding what to do next. Accepting or declining offers	Knowing some organisations treat you as their customer or VIP, although some don't	Working differently in future – where / when will you begin? Preparing for a new role
Considering a new role – what's important to you?	Maintaining or recovering your positive energy and preparing for disappointments	Telling me what you think. How did I do? Feedback, etc.

Postscript

If you have more questions or want to delve into a specific topic in a little more detail once you've read the relevant chapters, my website may help especially Tea Break — Heather Watt (https://www.heatherwatt.co.uk/tea-break).

Chapter One

Know your strengths and what's important to you

Be that hero

All good stories start with a hero, right? And now it's your turn to be *that* hero, although I recognise how tough that might be. Seeking a new role puts you front and centre stage in the spotlight, and that's not a comfortable place for everyone. Let's face it, the challenge of self-assessment and putting stuff into words that resonate with others can be a bit like sucking anchovies – an acquired taste. That's where I can help you, although first things first, let's get positive. On a count of three, try blowing away any traces of negativity and focus on all the great things that you've done… today, this week, in your career. One, two, three… **let's glow!**

Before we begin writing for others, let's write for ourselves

Most of us have a surprisingly good idea of what we do well (and what we do less well); after all, we've lived with the knowledge for most of our lives. Inevitably, the descriptors will have developed over time to become more detailed, perhaps even losing their sense of fun and impact.

Remember those early school reports, 'a bit of a comedian', 'a great performer', or 'enjoys finding out how things work', and the impact the comments had on you? More recently, it may be that other people have put you into their own words, 'tackles challenges with a sense of humour', 'commands an audience with ease', or 'brilliant engineer'. Now it's time to wind back time. How do you want to describe yourself? Are you a performer, or someone who commands an audience with ease? Which do you prefer?

You. In your own words

Let's begin with what you're good at first and then we'll move on to your values. It's time to make a list of three to five strengths. That's three to five strengths written in your own words (rather than corporate language) with the strongest one at the top of your list. Try to be selective; this is no place for FOMO. Be decisive and ask yourself: "Is this really a strength?"

You may find it helpful to record your ideas on the grid[1] on the next page. It may take a few attempts before you're happy with the result. Then, just to throw a spanner in the works, the priority order may change when you begin to focus on your strengths at work or in education (rather than strengths at home).

Alternatively, you may prefer to begin with your values (the things that you judge to be important in life) before listing your strengths. Later in the text, we'll consider how your strengths help you at work. Don't worry, you're not on your own, I'm here to help you and I've included lots of examples to support you with the tasks.

Top tip – Recording your progress by writing things down often helps you to see how far you've come and what you've changed.

---

1   We're all different and, if you're not one for writing in books (in case you spoil them), I recommend copying or reproducing the grid in your own style. Remember to keep track of what you've recorded, although it's only for you and by you, so it doesn't need to be 'picture perfect'.

My strengths in life

Write your ideas below

	1	
	2	
	3	
Potential substitution	4	
Potential substitution	5	

How my strengths help me at work

Next, let's focus on you at work (or in full-time study) with the strengths you've recorded above in mind. For example, if one of your strengths is having great conversations and chatting with people, how has that helped with communicating difficult messages to clients or colleagues at work, or to fellow students?

You may want to (or feel you need to) shift the language and phrases you use towards a more corporate style, although I'm encouraging you to keep your own unique identity. Remember to write for your audience as well as yourself. For example, who will read your CV or cover letter, and so on.

Back to basics – A four-step approach to knowing yourself better			
1	2	3	4
What I'm good at / my strengths	How my strengths help me at work	My values – what's important to me	What I value at work

✏️ My strengths at work

There are some 'worked examples' on the next page which may help you	1	
	2	
	3	
Potential substitution	4	
Potential substitution	5	

✏️ The things that are important to me (in life and at work)

	My values – how I live my life	My workplace values* – what's important to me at work
1		
2		
3		
4		
5		

* It may be that your values are your values and don't change from home to work – that's fine, although it's worth a few moments of reflection.

> **Top tip** – Try to be as true to yourself as you can be. This is for you and by you and it's not for sharing at this stage.

Some examples to help you

My strengths in life	**1**	Persistence, determination, doing what I say I'm going to do
	2	Creativity, thinking creatively, imagination, having good ideas
	3	Having great conversations, chatting with people
Potential substitution	**4**	Empathy and building rapport with people I don't know well
Potential substitution	**5**	A focus on facts and figures, understanding value for money

The next two alternatives are based on the same five strengths although different work environments:

My strengths in life	**1**	Getting things done / deadlines met, completing tasks with focus
	2	Inventing things or coming up with new ways of doing things
	3	Communicating messages in ways that aid understanding
Potential substitution	**4**	Engaging and influencing the team, succeeding in a team
Potential substitution	**5**	Achieving the best return on investments made, grasping P&L

My strengths in life	**1**	Getting things done / deadlines met, completing tasks with focus
	2	Creating a plant-based menu for a five-star hotel restaurant
	3	Using conversation to canvass client views and feedback
Potential substitution	**4**	Influencing clients to think differently about veganism
Potential substitution	**5**	Increasing sales by 'above average' percentages for the sector

	My values – how I live my life	My workplace values
1	Creating a sustainable environment	Recycling and reducing carbon footprint
2	Looking after my well-being	Being valued for my business contribution
3	Adventuring and trying out new things	Working at the leading edge of innovation
4	Creating or getting value for money	An ethical approach to doing business
5	Treating people with respect and empathy	An inclusive welcome every single time

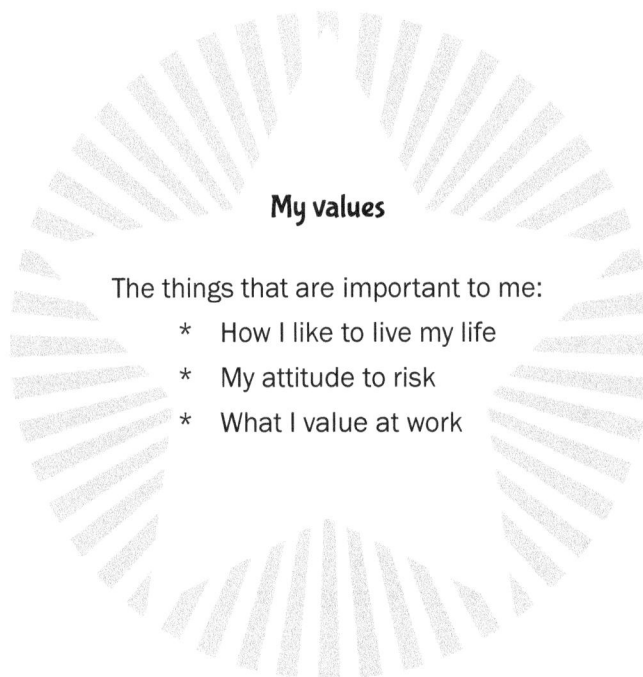

My values

The things that are important to me:

* How I like to live my life
* My attitude to risk
* What I value at work

Think results

Your strengths and what's important to you (your values) all play their part in what you achieve at work and beyond. It's good to get into the habit of recognising the contribution you made to a task (think of it as an output). In other words, begin to think about the result of your contributions, particularly as that's often greater than the effort expended. To put it another way, your achievements are the combination or product of your knowledge and your actions.

Successes

Employers want to hear your success stories and what's gone well. They want to understand what you've achieved before and how you went about it, because it's highly likely that you'll repeat that success for them – and perhaps even improve on it, with their additional encouragement and motivation. This is all about positive outcomes and wins.

From time to time, I read CVs that give me a laundry list of personal traits along the lines of reliable, friendly or punctual. Good to read, although this could be a description of most people in most organisations (to a greater or lesser extent). Are you a great communicator or are you simply chatty? Both descriptors offer insight, although neither tell me what's been achieved. I'd like to know more about how you used your communication skills to improve something. For example: "I delivered an influencing skills workshop, and the young audience complimented me on my style of communication – easy to follow."

Challenge yourself

I've created the following practical task to help you to pinpoint what makes you special and what you're likely to contribute to work. Once you've conquered the challenge, you'll have between six and nine unique achievements to work with based on your key strengths (the ones you've already identified on page 4). I'm encouraging you to think outside the box, which will be especially helpful if you're swapping your flying credentials for a career in social care.

Top tip – Recording your progress by writing things down often helps you to see how far you've come and what you've changed.

✏️ My top three strengths

My top three strengths (from page 4)	1	
	2	
	3	

Now I'm encouraging you to use your top three identified strengths and create work-based achievements to discuss on your CV and at interview. It's as easy as A, B, C

A. List three words (strengths) that best describe you / are most frequently used about you
B. For each of the three strengths in turn, highlight two or three different components, and
C. Now list two or three achievements that have contributed to each strength (remember to size or to include a metric)

I've provided a worked example to help you on the next page, although you are the only one who can select your top three strengths.

If you've already read page 4, you're likely to have identified your strengths, although you may be undecided about which three of the five possibles to finalise. If you've just started here, it's probably time to catch up. **Good Luck!**

> 💡 **Top tip** – STAR performance is a helpful structure when writing up your achievements and it's explained for you on the next page.

Example

If one of your top three strengths is confident communication, three noteworthy components of that might be (1) making presentations (2) public speaking (3) engaging a crowd and networking. The table below takes each component and suggests an achievement (output).

Strength No. 1 – Confident Communication	
Individual component	**Example achievement**
Making presentations	Delivered a three-day learning event for twelve colleagues via Microsoft Teams
Public speaking	Shared my experiences of remote working at a global leadership event for 100 franchisees
Engaging a crowd and networking	Hosted and facilitated an industry forum on sustainable packaging for fifty delegates

Structuring achievements

STAR – a useful acronym

Situation – What were the circumstances? Provide some context for the example.

Task – What did you need to do? Were you given the challenge or was it your idea?

Action – What did you do? How did you go about it?

Result – What was the outcome and what did you learn?

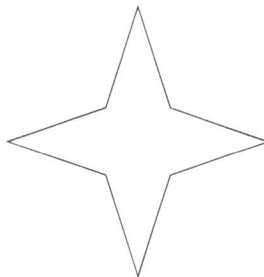

Turning strengths into achievements

Now it's your opportunity to make good use of your top three strengths and consider the components of each in turn. Then, like the cherry on the cake, the resulting achievement. No surprises, it may take a few attempts before you're happy with the outcome. It's likely that you'll want to extend these achievements a little when you come to tell your story and finalise your CV.

Example achievements

Confident Communication – three example components	Linking Confident Communication with Business Focus – three example achievements
Delivered a three-day learning event for twelve colleagues via Microsoft Teams	Delivered a learning event for twelve colleagues via Microsoft Teams, which reduced travel / subsistence costs by c£10K over the four days
Shared my experiences of remote working at a global leadership event for 100 franchisees	Shared my experiences of remote working at a global leadership event for 100 franchisees, to illustrate increased return on investment (ROI)
Hosted and facilitated an industry forum on sustainable packaging for fifty delegates	Hosted and facilitated an industry forum on sustainability for fifty delegates and secured £100K sponsorship towards future research

It's your turn to create some fabulous achievements based on your strengths combined with your work or life experiences. Remember, we're aiming for the most influential examples you're able to articulate, although it's more impactful if they're fairly recent (as the detail will be sharper in your mind and much easier to recollect at interview).

Top tip – Be brave and give it a go – after all, only you will see it. Remember to include some metrics.

My achievements

Your strength No. 1 ... what's top of your list?	
Component	Achievement (output)

Your strength No. 2 ... what's top of your list?	
Component	Achievement (output)

Your strength No. 3 ... what's top of your list?	
Component	Achievement (output)

Your strength No. 4 ... what's top of your list?	
Component	Achievement (output)

Broaden your audience

Here's one final point from me about writing up your achievements. Try to write in a language that'll resonate with as broad an audience as possible without losing impact. For me, that means avoiding unnecessary jargon, any sector-specific technical detail and obscure abbreviations, especially if you're hoping to switch career paths or sectors. For example, from maître d' to customer service manager, from pilot or sales director in aviation to customer experience lead in logistics, and so on.

Remember these achievements will be an integral part of your CV and recruitment discussions or interviews, so please make sure that they sparkle! There's more about tailoring your communication in chapter eight later in this text and creating a sparkling CV in Chapter Three.

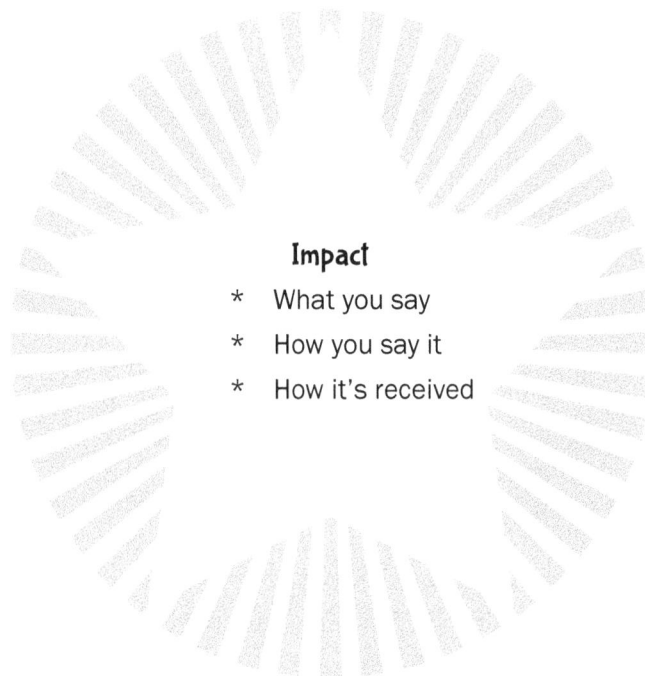

Impact
* What you say
* How you say it
* How it's received

> **Top tip** – Remember that an **achievement** is not just a statement of activity but the **result** or **what** you achieved, either at work, at home, or for your family and/or friends.

Chapter Two

Own your own story and tell it with conviction

"You can't go back and change the beginning,
but you can start where you are and change the ending."

Attributed to C. S. Lewis, although often debated

I've included this quote above because I use it frequently and successfully when I'm coaching to get conversations off to a positive start. It's got more clout than some of those platitudes like, 'what's done is done', and I love a bit of clout. The quote is relevant to telling your unique story!

Recap

It's likely that you've begun our adventure together with a challenge to identify your top three strengths, your values and some pithy achievements. I say 'likely' because you may have gone straight to Chapter Three as a CV rewrite was urgent and long overdue!

I encouraged you to come up with some recent examples of you putting these top three strengths to work for you. Hopefully, you now have some really clear achievements to boast about on your CV and at recruitment meetings or interviews. Put simply, this is the beginning of your story, the one to rehearse and get comfortable with. The one that boosts your confidence and self-belief.

Our stories provide insight into what's important to us and sometimes even set the boundaries for what we do and how we interact with others. They explain what we've done, where we've been and where we want to go. Stories are influential and help us demonstrate our values and expectations to others. That's why I've included stories and storytelling in a recruitment guide (just in case you were wondering), although they may not seem like an obvious choice. Read on to discover more about creating stories and storytelling to add impact.

Storytelling

The notion of storytelling in recruitment originated during some of my early coaching sessions with newly displaced (not quite unemployed) colleagues several decades ago. Eloquent speakers and great communicators (about all things engineering), until it came to talking about themselves. I needed to get them talking about themselves with the same degree of persuasiveness and influence as they applied to talking about bridges and trains!

It's evolved and grown since then, becoming a key element of how I support people like you through change. Together we can create fabulous and believable stories that link the different chapters of your life – work and home, education and work, dreams and aspirations. I'm not telling you this to blow my own trumpet, but to demonstrate how storytelling fits into your recruitment toolkit.

I'm here to help you compose your story and tell it with ease. Your story needs to flow through and around your career, your life, your hopes and dreams without interruption. Eventually, your story will be reflected in your CV, and every networking conversation or interview you have. Storytelling is an essential plank for communicating with other people. It's a dynamic medium and a great skill to master. And, like me, you'll soon develop your own unique style.

Great tales

Our stories define who we are and provide valuable context to how we behave. Imagine a life without English folklore heroes like Robin Hood, who is said to have redistributed the wealth of the rich to the poor in the fourteenth century, or the tales of the Arabian Nights told across Persia, Arabia, India and Asia for thousands of years. An early favourite of mine, *The Canterbury Tales* (Chaucer, 1400) provides a glimpse of life in the middle ages through the eyes of a group of pilgrims. We get to read *The Miller's Tale*, *The Cook's Tale*,

The Knight's Tale and many more, although six centuries later, I suspect the storytellers would include a blogger, a gamer and an astronaut, as well as all kinds of influencers.

Getting started

Some of the best stories are the ones you tell at the bus stop, in the supermarket queue or when you're introduced to somebody new at a party. It's less likely that you'll mask your feelings of joy that the bus is early, or the queue is fast-moving. You'll not bother with overly complicated sentences or professional jargon to describe your role as a software developer (or solutions architect) unless it's an industry event. Try thinking about your story and your career in its simplest form. Imagine telling your story to someone who doesn't have prior knowledge or insight into what you've done and what you want to do. "Hi, I'm Heather and I support people into work."

Remember that Artificial Intelligence (AI) can help

I'm thrilled that we have so many tools to help us write at our disposal, although we owe it to ourselves to use them wisely. I love that there are options to correct misspellings or prompt us to think again about sentence construction. From time to time, I've taken up an offer of help from a widget that's appeared on my screen (there are many), yet the suggestions are often 'too flowery' or 'over-emphasised' for my style of writing. I recognise that there are options for learning (on both sides), although I'm beginning to hear tales of CVs being disregarded as, 'clearly written by a bot or AI generated'. Only you will know, although remember, you will need to live up to the reputation or story you've created at interview – enough said?

Compiling your story

Sometimes we need to modify the content or our stories to suit the audience, but that comes later. Right now, I'm keen to get you thinking about your story in your own words. It's likely that if you're reading this, you've already made some progress with identifying your strengths (page 4). Together with some strong examples of your achievements (page 11), these strengths and what's important to you (your values) are key to your story.

Another way to think about your story comes from your reputation – what do people remember about you? Are you the 'doer' and the 'organiser', or are you the 'problem solver'? And come to think of it, what do you *want* people to remember about you? Now there's a leap forward!

Reputation			
1	2	3	4
What's my reputation currently?	What do people say about me?	What do I want people to say about me?	What do I want people to remember about me?

Keep it simple

Sometimes our stories aren't always clear to us, even though we're the main protagonists. Frequently, that's because, as the hero of our own story, we're focused too much on the detail or precision. Our stories become too complicated for simple explanations or the audience we've attracted. Then we overcompensate with too much justification (and, dare I say, padding).

From time to time, it's the questions we're asked that give rise to confusing responses. Imprecise questions (particularly at interview) can lead us to waffle until we're interrupted or asked politely to speed up. If you're clear on your story, you can at least avoid *that* rabbit warren. You get to tell your story whatever the question and whatever the quality of the question.

Real-life example

This reminds me of my time interviewing with one executive who frequently asked candidates for a 'potted history' of their life and career. Their puzzled expressions said it all – what's a potted history, for goodness' sake? Then he'd explain that he was seeking a simple career explanation, but didn't need to know about swimming certificates. He was not for coaching but that didn't stop me. He'd been asking similar questions throughout his career and wasn't going to budge. A pity because he wasn't helping his candidates to be the best candidate they knew how to be.

Brevity

The moral of this tale is stay true to your story, even when poor interview technique (or a poor interviewer) intervenes. And remember, if you're unsure of the level of detail required, err on the side of caution and brevity. Interviewers will always ask you to elaborate if that's needed.

Understanding and telling your story			
1	2	3	4
Stand out in a competitive jobs market for all the right reasons	You are the hero of your story – how you use your strengths to win the day	Where you've been, what you've done & where you want to go	The hero's journey – your adventure & your victory – what a transformation

Uncomplicated progress

The example over the page is a way of making some tangible links between a master's in human biology, an early and successful career in retail management, a logical move via a project into recruitment and a desire to remain there. And even a move into HR. This story (which is not my story, by the way) brings all the different elements together. It brings life to a list of somehow unrelated statements. There's a vastly different example that explains a slightly disjointed career on the next page (page 19).

> **Top tip** – Remember that your story links the different chapters of your life with your aspirations – it's a great way to communicate with your audience.

Example – My story

> *My education was rooted in the sciences, although some early part-time work in retail persuaded me to take a different path. I've been a fully-fledged store section manager for the past couple of years and I've won several awards for team engagement and increased profitability from improved margins.*
>
> *Right now, I'm halfway through a twelve-month secondment to a head office role, working on a redesign of the careers site with a fully integrated testing platform. I'm keen to continue my career in recruitment once the assignment completes, because I'm enjoying selling this great business to potential colleagues. I'm even thinking of studying towards my CIPD qualifications.*

Over to you

It may seem ages since you began to identify your strengths on page 4 or you wrote up some achievements on pages 11, but now it's time to weave them into your story. Using the example above as a model, what is the simplest form of your story? Once you've got that clear, the rest of your challenge becomes easier. Remember to include all the twists and turns that explain (briefly) any changes of direction and keep the spotlight well and truly fixed on your successes – your positive outcomes. You'll be great.

Aspirations and ambitions

Remember that your story is as much about where you've been, what you've done and your strengths and achievements as it is about where you want to go – your ambitions. In the example above, the concluding phrase, "I'm even thinking of studying towards my CIPD qualifications" hints at what comes next.

> **Top tip** – Remember this is your story created by you in your words and about the things you're happy to share.

Different ways of presenting your notes

Here's an example that shows how some apparently disjointed elements come together and tell your story. Rather than racking your brains to remember every single casual or part-time opportunity you encountered as a student or in your early career, think in terms of a portfolio of experience.

My story			
1	**2**	**3**	**4**
Casual late night bar work & part-time fashion studies	Low paid intern role in millinery, bar & events work	Wedding venue co-ordinator & part-time floristry course	Creating tiaras from fresh flowers and venue manager

Another example – My story

My interests and greatest achievements have always been rooted in art and fashion, although my early career was a bit haphazard. Lots of different roles in hospitality, gaining as much knowledge as I could came together. I created an enviable experience portfolio to run alongside my artistic talents and interests.

The wedding venue was where it all came together. I'm delighted to have carved out a career for myself in events management. It provides a fabulously creative environment, which relies on watertight administration, as well as innovation. I've certainly needed all those strengths to survive the past year.

I'm excited for what the future holds for me as I begin to think about branching out on my own for some of the time.

Back to the future

An alternative approach to telling your story, which you may prefer, is to look forward. This is your opportunity to project yourself into the future and think about which direction your story could take. A word of caution: this approach relies on a very clear aspiration or set of ambitions. You may also find that this future-focus approach helps you to visualise and tell your current story. It'll certainly provide some insights into your aspirations and expectations, and it may even help you to articulate your dream role.

My story – the next chapter

* *What will my adventure be?*
* *What challenges will I encounter?*
* *What decisions will I need to make?*
* *What will my transformation be?*

Your story, your aspirations, your CV

I hope that you've enjoyed spending some time thinking about yourself, whichever approach you selected – looking to the future and your aspirations, or reflecting on what you've achieved already, or a combination of both. Now that you've mastered your strengths and storytelling, it's time to thread that story through your CV. It's time to capture the great things you've done in your life so far and want to do next. Let's use them to secure a new role that works for you!

Top tip – Your focus should be on you and your new employer. Try to learn from any previous mistakes (or shabby treatment) and leave it all behind. This is your future.

What do you want to do next? What are your aspirations?

Write your ideas here

_____

_____

_____

_____

_____

_____

_____

_____

_____

_____

_____

_____

_____

_____

_____

_____

Top tip – Remember to keep your story uncomplicated and your achievements exciting and fresh. Hang on in there!

Chapter Three

Creating a compelling CV

You may have recognised that much of the preceding two chapters is dedicated to preparing you for this chapter and creating a fabulous CV. There's much in the news about CVs being overtaken by technology, although right now, we're still hearing about students being asked for a CV when applying for part-time barista work or volunteering.

There's a lot in this chapter and I hope that I've made it easy for you to follow. Some feedback on my earlier draft suggested that I appeared to have lost my sense of humour in this chapter. Apologies in advance if you feel that's the case, although in my defence, this is such a critical element of your recruitment toolkit to get right. **No gimmicks!**

The term Curriculum Vitae (more recently CV) can be translated from Latin as, 'course of (one's) life'. Three years' Latin study at school just came into its own. CV has become the broad catch-all to describe your work, educational and professional achievements, along with your strengths. It's a critical self-marketing asset. Frequently, jobseekers are asked for a two-page CV. For me, that's a couple of sides of A4 with realistic margins. More about that later in the text. Some cultures favour a résumé, which tends to be a briefer description (possibly just one side of A4).

What you did

It's no surprise that a CV is not a JD (job description) – it's about you and what you've *done* rather than a (usually) poorly written laundry list of what you're *expected* to do. If there are tasks and activities on your JD that you didn't do (or didn't enjoy doing) then please remember to leave them off your CV. Conversely, you get to include all your achievements that weren't included in your JD!

Gather your ingredients

Working on your CV can be like preparing rich fruit cake. I recommend learning and understanding the basic technique and getting all the ingredients together in one place before practising the recipe. In other words, assemble what you're going to need and think about the overall image you want to create. A plate of French fancies or a steamed syrup sponge? An accomplished leader or a wannabe popstar? I recommend including your future ambitions and likely direction in that overall image as well. You need to be true to yourself yet appeal to your new audience.

Quick recap

Remember the exercise on identifying and describing your strengths and achievements in Chapter One? You'll need that detail now, as well as your story from Chapter Two. If you didn't manage to complete the tasks and need a CV in a hurry, remember to focus on your strengths and what you've achieved when you're writing. Then catch up when you've got time.

Now it's time to tell your story and weave it into your CV. Let's begin with your profile, the shortest version of your story (about three to five lines of text). The profile becomes your 'capsule wardrobe' of words – concise, curated, coordinated and sustainable. Your profile sets the scene for what's to come and it's a great reminder of what to say when your mind goes blank at interview.

Let's get started

1. Go on, be honest, when did you last review your CV?
2. And, hand on heart, did it wow you?
3. Did it truly reflect the person you are and want to be?

If you've answered 'no' to questions two and/or three, then it's time for a CV makeover.

> **Top tip** – Remember this is your story and your CV, not someone else's. Be proud to own your achievements.

Making time

I recognise that, if you're reading this, it's highly likely that you simply want to get the best CV you can as quickly as possible and here I am shouting, "Stop!" Or, at least, "Pause." The best CVs are written when they are not needed. If the recruiter has given you twenty-four hours to submit your best effort, then you have four potential options to choose from. I'd be inclined to try for the second option and then possibly the fourth, although I'll leave you to decide.

1. Quickly add a few details to your existing CV and hope for the best
2. Negotiate for a little more time, consider what's needed and focus on delivery
3. Exclaim that's not nearly long enough and decline
4. Revise your CV in line with your emerging story and aspirations – whatever it takes

CV components

There are endless opportunities to use or create flamboyant CV designs online, although less really is more. There's a good starting point and a little more detail on the next page. I recommend an uncomplicated template, which deliberately excludes tables, horizontal lines and other graphics, as these aren't always compatible with all recruitment systems. If you're a graphic artist or fashion designer, you may prefer something more creative, although you can achieve that with spot colour and font choices. Think of the simplicity and sophistication of, for example, The White Company, which gained success through its ease of choice.

Personal profile

It's more than likely that you've done your research, and considered best advice, yet you're still in two minds about whether to include a profile on your CV or not. I encourage a profile section for several reasons. Not least because it helps you to focus on who you are and what you offer – whether that's to your existing or a potential employer, or someone who's on the lookout for a new perspective from a speaker or a commentator.

What to include

Sometimes it's helpful to think about your profile as your 'elevator pitch'. In other words, how you describe yourself when time is short. Remember to focus on your unique attributes; "Consistently achieves financial targets" says much more about you than "hardworking". Similarly, "An accomplished strategist and marketing communications leader" sets the tone for what's to come. Try to avoid unnecessary jargon, which may distance some readers early on.

> **Top tip** – This guide is about being the best candidate and securing a new role, although a sparkling CV may also help you to secure ad hoc project work or speaking assignments.

Example CV layout with notes

Name

Contact information – email and mobile as a minimum
Location – where it's relevant, could be a postcode, town or region

Profile:

A few sentences to describe what you are all about and the contribution you will make to my[2] business. Use the best descriptor of your job, profession and organisational level. It's perfectly acceptable to include abbreviations for recognised roles, e.g., C-suite, CEO, MD, CIO, CFO, CPO or HRD.

> It may be helpful to ask yourself which three strengths (from the Chapter One tasks) are you keen to include as a minimum? Confident and influential communications? Commercial savvy and business focus? Try to include insights to your personality, attitudes and reputation or aspirations, then weave into other sections of the CV.

---

2   'My' in this example refers to a potential employer.

Key achievements:

Strengths and/or key skills followed by relevant and recent achievements that demonstrate them (aim for at least five separate achievements to demonstrate breadth). You've made great progress with your achievements already, although you may have others to include now that you've got to this point.

Example key achievements:
- Delivered a learning event for twelve colleagues via Microsoft Teams, which reduced travel/subsistence costs by c£10K over the four days
- Shared my experiences of remote working at a global leadership event for 100 franchisees, to illustrate increased return on investment (ROI)
- Hosted and facilitated an industry forum on sustainability for fifty delegates and secured £100K sponsorship towards future research

---

Experience:

Your Job title(s)
Organisation   *Dates*

Synopsis of your role/the organisation, e.g., turnover or complexity, team size, etc.
- Aim for between five and nine activities that capture the spirit of each role
- Include a chronology of employment successes written in output terms along with measures of success, e.g., decreased costs by X%, saving £X in first quarter
- Try not to duplicate what you've already covered in key achievements
- Aim to provide detailed information for at least the past five years
- Remember to use strong, active verbs and keep phrases crisp
- Early career roles require less explanation and detail
- Aim to include at least two roles on the first page to demonstrate breadth
- Use bullet points that open with a relevant verb to make activities shine
- Recent college leavers should consider how best to present their success stories

[If you've just left full-time education, remember your experience comprises volunteering, part-time roles and even hobbies or interests that have enhanced your skills, e.g., organising, communicating, delivering excellent customer service.]

Credentials:

Professional and academic achievements or learning relevant to your chosen career path.

CV layout:

Remember to observe the following protocols to create impact:
- Keep to a readable font size (ideally 11 or 12 point) and style to aid readability
- Leave space between sections, keep margins normal to moderate
- Position what you write in the centre of the page and leave a sensible border
- Try not to overcrowd the page and allow the words to pop from the background
- Write in the past tense, i.e., what you did/achieved – exceptions being profile/ current role
- Keep bullet points to either one line or just over one line to create impact
- Begin achievements and activities with strong verbs, e.g., transformed, led, saved

Example Personal Profile

An influential HR consultant, writer and inspirational coach, I collaborate with groups and individuals to make their change aspirations a reality. Noted for delivery as well as innovation and creativity, I measure my success in terms of performance improvements and lasting partnerships. [42 words]

Combining HR, graphic design and editorial advice

Content is only half of the story and, although some of my colleagues will doubtless disagree, I work to the principle that structure, layout and impact are as important as content. There's much to suggest that CVs are frequently reviewed by bots to algorithms rather than humans, concluding that it's only the content that really matters.

There are some amazing recruitment systems around right now, although even systems appreciate clarity and white space between points. Bullet points should ease readability and comprehension. Try to think of margins as 'print free zones' and a frame to show off what you have to say.

Using vocabulary wisely

It's a good idea to get familiar with some strong verbs that don't need lots of adjectives to shore them up, and remember to include metrics, e.g., volumes, savings, increased sales or margins and performance improvements to add strength to the points you are making. You may find it helpful to make a list of some descriptive verbs you like the sound of, to add colour to your CV and bring out your personality. I'm thinking of verbs like launched, influenced, modernised and redesigned. And here are a few worked examples to get your creative juices flowing.

Examples

1. "**Transformed** business processes and delivered £50K of efficiencies within 12 months" is a lot more insightful and stronger than, "successfully updated business processes"
2. "**Reduced** overhead costs to the business by 20% resulting from just in time learning" tells a more convincing story than, "reorganised training"
3. "**Doubled** customer satisfaction scores to 70% by halving queue times/introducing self-service options" is clearly an improvement on, "introduced customer self-service"

Now it's your turn to draft your profile – what can you write about yourself in up to seventy words? There are no rules, although remember to use vocabulary wisely. Too many adjectives? Time to try a new verb.

✏️ **Write your ideas here**

Your Personal Profile [50 – 70 words]	
99	[there's an example on the previous page]

The following example illustrates how one of my individual clients composed their profile to capture what they aspired to do as well as what they could offer in the meantime.

Another Example [69 words]

A confident student pilot with a reputation for getting things done, I am seeking an opportunity that will challenge my strengths and enable me to develop new skills alongside my passion for flying. My goal is to fly planes commercially, although right now I bring commitment, excellent organisational and leadership capability. I work well in a team, where I can use my influential communication skills to interact with others.

💡 **Top tip** – Remember to use realistic margins and resist overcrowding the page. Create a clear border all around your words like a picture frame enhancing a priceless piece of art!

Output focus

We've already established that your CV isn't a description of what's expected of you, but a demonstration of what you've achieved. That's what you did and the outcome, rather than the range of tasks anticipated, often called responsibilities on your JD (although I prefer to work to accountabilities, but that's for another time).

Let's get writing

I'm suggesting that you consider this first draft of your CV as a blueprint. Depending on how much you have to say, you may already have a good idea of how much space you need to get your story across to your audience. Let's hope two sides of A4 is sufficient. And don't forget the 'print free zone', the picture frame. There's much written about a two-page limit. If that means very narrow margins and extraordinarily small typeface, I recommend opting for three. Just one paragraph on the third page may suggest poor planning. This is where your formatting skills may be stretched.

Example strengths and achievements

- **Excellent communication skills** – presents written and spoken material with ease and to suit the needs of my audiences, including customers
- **Focus and commitment to achieving objectives** – A level and Duke of Edinburgh Silver Award successes, included six months volunteering with a local charity
- **Well-developed organisation skills** – balanced the stringent demands of A level study, flying hours and pilot exams to achieve successful outcomes
- **Confident and outgoing** – used my ability to interact with a broad range of personalities through education, cadet training, volunteering and pilot training
- **Pragmatic and solutions focused** – achieved my objective to learn to fly, successfully completing my first flying lesson aged fifteen

---

Credentials

There are a few different approaches. Traditional headings have been Education and Qualifications or Education and Training. More recently, Education and Vocational Learning or Credentials have been adopted. My best advice to you is to use the descriptor that best aligns with your achievements. I'll exaggerate to make the point by encouraging you to avoid the term Qualifications then only listing a one-day customer service workshop from ten years ago.

The small print

You'll have noticed that I don't mention passports, driving licences or hobbies as *essential* elements of a CV and this is easily explained. I don't see the point of taking up valuable space on a CV with "references available upon request" or huge amounts of text given over to referees' contact details, which have a limited shelf life. Some public sector processes require potential referees along with other safeguarding information, although that's typically uploaded as part of the application process. Similarly, passport details and any compulsory qualifications, e.g. HGV driving licence.

Hobbies, interests and keeping busy

Hobbies and interests may demonstrate individual breadth, although there have been times when I've fought against the notion that the captain of the rugby fifteen will make a great engineer. Keeping busy is critical for jobseekers whose employment status has waned and learning new skills like breadmaking or creating children's stories came into their own in lockdown. Practising yoga may highlight your agility, although how relevant is that to an HR Director role?

The following example creates a neat way of signing off on full-time education while demonstrating breadth and ambition. This was a sentence created by one of my clients as they entered the jobs market for the first time. It worked for them as they wanted to show that they had a plan and had something to chat about at interview.

Example

> *I have many interests, although my commitment to job search, together with flying and achieving success in my pilot's exams (not to mention learning to drive) just leave time for me to hit the gym and follow my favourite football team.*

I'm going to leave the decision of what to include with you, although please consider the space you have available and if the addition will add impact to your expertise or story.

Quick recap

Understanding my strengths and values	✓
Clarifying my recent achievements and key skills	✓
Rehearsing and telling my story	✓
Understanding what the future holds for me	✓
Compiling an engaging CV that truly represents me	✓
Seeking early feedback and proofreading	✓

What's next?

Your CV is not an end, although it's an essential self-marketing tool and will certainly be required when you're ready to apply for a new role or canvass feedback on your consulting skills. Remember to update your online presence (your socials) as soon as your new CV is complete. It's vital that your CV and any other channels are up to date, especially LinkedIn.

Updating recruiters and job sites

Most recruiters love an updated CV and it's a good idea to circulate yours at the earliest opportunity. Help them to help you by adding a simple footer with your name and date on the second page to signal change. It's a simple transaction that doesn't need huge amounts of explanation about what's added or deleted, "I've given myself a positive makeover and I know you'll agree it's so much more impactful than the previous CV."

Video

Now that you've created such a great CV and you're comfortable with your story, consider how best to take your self-marketing to another level. What else can you do to promote your capabilities and stand out to potential employers for all the right reasons? It's time to evaluate the benefits of making a short video. You can use it to enhance your online presence or attach it to emails when contacting recruiters and others in your network.

Video content

I recommend revisiting your personal profile (your elevator pitch), as this will become the foundation for your video pitch. Add in a couple of achievements and a whistle-stop tour of critical experience and relevant credentials. All this, plus a summary of your aspirations and in a time window of less than two minutes, what's not to enjoy? Remember to look at the camera, smile as often as you can manage and engage your audience. This is your opportunity to tell your story and stand out for all the right reasons. **Try to smile!**

The rehearsal (video)

- Recognise what you want to cover and rehearse
- Try to avoid parrot-like delivery or (obviously) reading from notes
- Use a good quality camera on a mobile device to practise
- Review and start again, until you're satisfied with the result
- Decide whether to purchase or borrow a desktop tripod/light ring to enhance impact
- Invite feedback from those who know you well
- Remember you're not trying to win a BAFTA

Your LinkedIn profile

It's a good idea to keep your messages to market consistent. I appreciate that you may feel you don't have any more time (or the inclination) to update your LinkedIn profile just as you've completed your new CV. Once you begin to circulate your CV, remember that your LinkedIn profile needs to be just as sharp, and the two elements of your self-marketing need to be in harmony. I advise against including your entire CV on your LinkedIn profile. Better to use your profile to gain interest in what you might have to offer.

Remember to update your profile as soon as you have new information. Delete what's no longer available as a minimum. Then, when you have a little more time, you can update a section at a time. I'd always encourage you to consider how much personal and work information you want in the public domain. Similarly, previous posts or comments. Posting relevant articles or stories on LinkedIn and commenting on posts of interest to you helps to raise awareness, although remember that you're seeking positive publicity!

If you don't already have a LinkedIn profile, it's easy to set up. All you need is a clear and current photograph ready to upload, and a copy of your CV from which to work. I recommend using the space behind your photograph wisely to ensure that you stand out from the crowd. Maybe add a royalty-free image or one that you've taken yourself that sums you up or makes you smile! The possibilities are endless. **Have fun!**

> **Top tip** – Remember to get a second opinion / proofreader to comment, although that doesn't mean you're obliged to make any changes suggested. They may just provide food for thought.

CVs – further reading from my Tea Break blog ... follow the links

- Your CV, a "pen picture" of you — Heather Watt: https://www.heatherwatt.co.uk/tea-break/2024/10/11/your-cv-a-pen-picture-of-you
- Be brave, be consistent and be yourself — Heather Watt: https://www.heatherwatt.co.uk/tea-break/2024/7/13/be-brave-be-consistent-and-be-yourself
- Silk flowers on my cakes – no way! — Heather Watt: https://www.heatherwatt.co.uk/tea-break/2024/3/15/silk-flowers-on-my-cakes-no-way-1
- When a good CV becomes great — Heather Watt: https://www.heatherwatt.co.uk/tea-break/2024/1/7/when-a-good-cv-becomes-great-1
- CVs past, present and future — Heather Watt: https://www.heatherwatt.co.uk/tea-break/2021/11/22/cvs-past-present-and-future
- Let's talk CVs and bees — Heather Watt: https://www.heatherwatt.co.uk/tea-break/2021/5/21/lets-talk-cvs-and-bees
- Great story. Great CV. Great performance. — Heather Watt: https://www.heatherwatt.co.uk/tea-break/2020/7/28/great-story-great-cv-great-performance
- Thinking outside of the box ... or is it the jam jar? — Heather Watt: https://www.heatherwatt.co.uk/tea-break/2020/6/9/thinking-outside-of-the-box-or-is-it-the-jam-jar
- Be outstanding. Practise out loud. — Heather Watt: https://www.heatherwatt.co.uk/tea-break/2020/1/14/practise-out-loud-its-the-essence-of-personal-success

Top tip – Try not to water down the impact of your new CV by leaving your old one posted on your socials or with headhunters. Remember to keep all profiles current and consistent.

Chapter Four

Understand your / any limits to flexibility

It's often so much easier to get to understand your limitations to flexibility well in advance, so at least you know what you might be giving up or trading when the time comes. You'll need to dig deep and be truthful to yourself. The effort you put in now will also save you some time when you are offered a role and need to make some decisions quickly.

I'm encouraging you to think about what's important to you, what's negotiable and what's not. Once you're clear on your expectations, it should help you to refine your job search criteria and avoid wasted time on chasing unrealistic dreams.

I'm all in favour of dreaming big, as long as it's just that – a big role, with fabulous opportunities and a bumper reward package. Beware of 'honey traps' designed to lure you into thinking that you can't own your own future unless you travel impractical distances, for unrealistic rewards. A few ideas to get your started.

Topic	Things to consider
Minimum / maximum working hours	Minimum may be relevant to hourly paid roles and maximum may be influenced by family or study. There may be portfolio career considerations.
Working pattern	As above, plus what you know you can realistically cope with – late nights / early mornings, weekends, etc.
Realistic salary minimum	This is not just about the right salary for the right role. Think dream role although poor remuneration, etc.

Principal work location	How realistic is the location and the journey? Think M25 or other motorway madness, public transport in winter, cost of travel, etc.
Working remotely	To what extent have you experienced WFH (working from home) and how was it? What did you enjoy / dislike? Dream or disaster?
Travel frequency	Staying away from home – dream or disaster? To what extent is a global, international, regional role realistic for you?
Job level	In many ways, the job level and the job content are intertwined, but if running the show is important to you then stick with it.
Job content	What are the 'must haves' – if you're a front of house manager, how will you flourish in a behind-the-scenes role? Excited to try something new?
Job title and status	What's your ideal in terms of recognition? Try not to be shy – how important is manager or director in your job title?
Learning opportunities	What personal development needs do you hope will be fulfilled?
✏️ Add your ideas here	

Chapter Five

Stay in touch with your networks

Networking in its simplest form is what we all do via our social channels to stay in touch with our friends or family and their news through Facebook or Instagram. You may already have taken this to another level by engaging with a professional networking group or online communities like LinkedIn. Perhaps you're simply good at staying connected with people you like, or people like you. Whatever your motivations, networking takes people and effort. It takes time to do it well and it's an investment of time.

Networking
· People and effort
· Shared interests
· Interactivity and collaboration
· Conversations
· Influential communications
· Face to face and digital

Give it a chance

You'll already have your own ideas about networking, I'm certain. If you've tried networking in the context of work or your profession and it's not your cup of tea, then I'm encouraging you to give it another try. It's worth bearing in mind that this isn't always about how many contacts you have, but the quality of your interactions with them. Remember to keep connections up to date and be sure to sustain the conversations. All too often when things are going well or we're busy, it's our business and professional networks that suffer from a lack of attention. Over time, you'll get to know how best to keep your networks going and how best to support others.

Extending your reach

Whether you've thousands of followers already or you're at the beginning of your business networking journey, it's a good idea to let your network know when you're needing to make change happen. I'd be surprised if your networks weren't keen to support you and, sometimes, they can even ease the pressure when it feels that there's simply no time for anything. In the same way that you help others through the tough times, they help you.

Influential conversations

The great thing about networking is that you get to decide what you want to share and how much you want to share. I'm not here to advise you what to share, although it's always a good idea not to overshare in a work or business context. Try not to write about or post something that detracts from, rather than enhances your professionalism. It's a good idea to recognise what you want to find out from your network and how you want to do that, as well as what you are keen to advertise.

Reputation

There are some questions below that are worth considering, as they will help you to build your personal brand, whether that's online or in person. Like all superstars, you can manage your reputation. You can take control of your own PR, and you can enlist the support of your network. You get to own your own future.

> **Top tip** – Try to get into the habit of keeping in touch and collaborating. Share the celebrations, not just the commiserations. Networking isn't just for the tough times.

Reputation
• What is my reputation currently? • What do people say about me? • What do I want people to say about me? • What do I want people to remember about me?

Top tip – Remember to avoid confrontation and negative comments – the genie never goes back in the bottle.

Chapter Six

Study your market

You may find it helpful to work on this chapter and the next chapter in parallel.

Introduction

I'm writing this as we all get ready to embrace 2025; hopefully a more positive year ahead for everyone. Whatever your personal or business circumstances – and recognising that some of my audience may be seeking promotion – it's a good idea to understand where you'll flourish. It's time to think creatively and research your different markets.

This chapter is really my placeholder to remind me to encourage you to do your research. You can put as much or as little time into this activity as floats your boat, although it's likely that the more you put in, the more you'll benefit. Surprisingly, I don't have a huge amount of content to share here because there are so many variations, but I've created the following checklist of good ideas to get you on the right track. I'm sure you'll think of more.

✏️ **Write your ideas in the boxes after each question**

> 💡 **Top tip** – Market research is a fabulous investment of your time and energy, and it's free of charge. What are you waiting for?

Where are the growth opportunities?

It's a good idea to consider which sectors appear to be thriving. I'm encouraging you to be open-minded at this point in time. High Street retail is challenging right now, although if you've great store retail expertise, online could just be your golden ticket to success. For example, if online shopping and delivery options (logistics) are booming, then try to put aside any negativity stemming from your current circumstances at this early stage.

Which roles are in demand?

You may come across 'new' roles that have become more popular as a result of current or recent trends. For example, these may be roles associated with health and social care since the pandemic. It's a good idea to map both the private and public sectors, even though your experience may be rooted in just one of the sectors.

Which organisations are recruiting?

Again, I'm promoting a factual approach (rather than an emotional one). For example, there may be some less than prestigious brands out there recruiting, which you later discover treat their colleagues like VIPs. Aim for a comprehensive list based on feedback from your networks (including recruiters).

Which sectors appear most significant to you?

Considering all you have to offer an employer, e.g., strengths, experience, interests, personality and qualifications, where are you going to target your search? You may have a plan B in mind, or you may decide to rank sectors in order of significance.

Which geographies/locations appear most significant?

Although relocation may not be practical or needed, it's well worth understanding and mapping areas of significance or interest, if only to acknowledge the rise in remote or more flexible working arrangements. Perhaps you've been living or working by the coast in hospitality and opportunities are inland.

What's next?

What are you going to follow up?

You can use this space for your notes.

_____

_____

_____

_____

_____

_____

_____

_____

_____

_____

_____

_____

_____

_____

_____

_____

_____

_____

_____

_____

Chapter Seven

Pursue only jobs that interest you

You may find it helpful to work on this chapter and the previous chapter in parallel.

Scientist or artist?

It's likely that we'll all have slightly different views on this point, although the more opportunities you follow up, the more your chances of success will improve. It's also worth considering that the more recruitment activities you engage with, the more disappointments you'll encounter. It's likely that your preferred approach will be determined by your interests. Are you the scientist or the artist? Whatever your preferences, you'll need to be strong and prepare for some disappointments.

No time for sitting on the fence

You wouldn't expect me to sit on the fence over this point (and I won't), although I want to provide some context to my advice. I'm encouraging you to focus on the opportunities that really interest you and the jobs that more closely match what you can offer. I'm all for you pushing the boundaries and demonstrating that you have transferrable skills or could grow into the role at a different organisational level. I'm less keen on you feeling obligated to apply for a role that won't stretch you, especially if it's in a sector you're not keen to explore.

Invest your time in what you want

This chapter is all about encouraging you to ignore the opportunities that don't seem to align with your interests and strengths, in favour of spending more time on those that do. Applications or cover letters done well are time consuming. You'll need to nail the conversations with recruiters and demonstrate a match, and there'll be questions to complete online as a minimum. And that's before you've got to all of the comings and goings of keeping up to date with progress. It'll be much easier to remain upbeat when you're discussing or writing about roles that genuinely excite you.

Nobody enjoys cold mashed potato

Mental agility is one thing but trying to demonstrate interest in a role for the sake of it can be like eating cold mashed potato. It'll keep you alive, but it's not very pleasant. Ask yourself the question, "Am I ready to hear that the hiring manager saw through my explanations?" and then make your decision. The jobs market is tough right now and you'll need to shine. Dump the façade and focus on what you enjoy.

Be kind to yourself

It's easy to get caught up in the moment and listen to the voices urging you to apply for just about every opportunity that grabs your attention. You know, the ones that ask, "What've you got to lose?" This is often where negativity begins to creep in. Sometimes it's compounded by financial worries and lapses of confidence. When you're desperate for a new role, it's easy to allow anxiety to hamper your progress. Somehow you feel that you need to be doing something, although it may not be the right thing. I'm here to help you to turn that around.

Do the right things well

Here are a few ideas for you to try out – let's make some lists and remember to keep your strengths at the front of your mind. Remember to communicate the outcomes with your network and make sure your CV reflects any new developments.

Transferability – my strengths, my skills and my experience

What I contribute now (recently)	How it could translate elsewhere
Managing regional and remote teams in the UK travel sector, plus supporting some franchisees	Franchise management in health & social care or regional retail management

Sectors that interest me	Sectors that I'm less keen to explore

Jobs I'm interested in exploring	Jobs I'm keen to avoid

My ideal organisation – what's important to me

Chapter Eight

Invest time in tailoring your communication

I'm encouraging you to get the best possible response to what you write and submit to potential employers or recruiters. I'm sure, like me, sometimes you smile, or other times flinch at how people address you in emails and other correspondence. I'm always pleased to read that my name is spelled correctly, although I prefer a simple, "Hello" to incorrectly spelled family names.

Make it personal

Before you hurry to circulate your CV or upload your application, remember to find out what you can about your audience. Sometimes it's a challenge to unearth the name of a specific recruiter or recipient of your application, although I recommend giving it a go in the first place.

Impact

In some ways the graphic on the next page is all you need to remember when you're communicating with others. I like the **impact** of the graphic. For me, it conjures up **colour**, even though it's black and grey!

> **Top tip** – And now it's back to reality, as I qualify my best advice, "Just say hello, if you can't remember my name."

Impact
* What you say
* How you say it
* How it's received

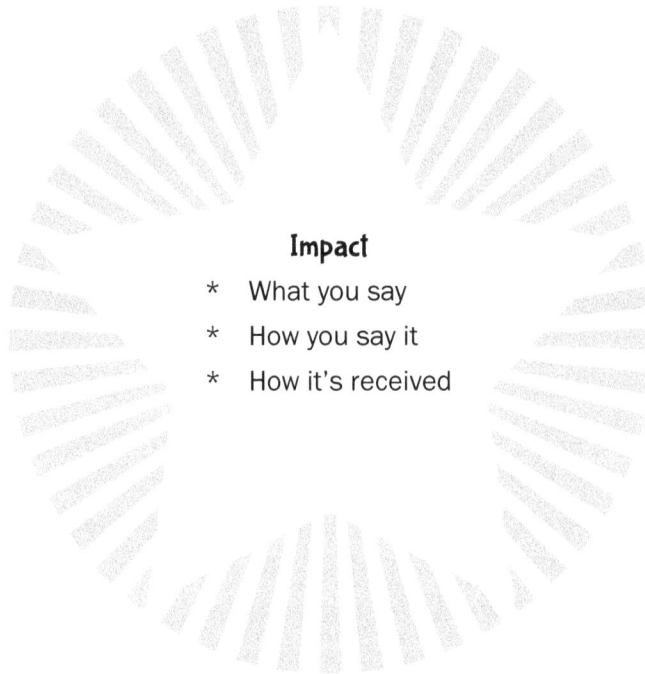

Write for yourself and for your audience

In the first chapter of this guide, I urged you to describe your strengths in your own words. It's good to be able to express yourself in words and phrases you recognise; language that resonates with you and helps to describe who you are. Once you're happy with what you've got, it will be so much easier to translate into what I'm calling 'business acceptable' language. And, of course, acceptable language varies from business to business – what's acceptable in gaming and film production may irritate the hell out of corporate compliance or finance.

Apply

I'm the biggest fan of uncomplicated application processes that enable the candidate and recruiter or hiring manager to come together with the least possible fuss or confusion. In their simplest form, modern applications usually comprise of your CV, either emailed or uploaded to a recruitment system. If you are working with a third-party recruiter or a headhunter, they may ask you for some additional information or a supporting statement.

Reflect the brief

There's unlikely to be a standard format and, to be honest, they could legitimately request copies of certifications or qualifications or a 250-word account of how you match the job criteria. The best advice here is to be clear about the requirements and the timeframe. Then complete the brief to the best of your talents, remembering that, if you are recycling or repurposing existing material, every word should reflect the new brief (and not the old one).

Covering letters and emails

It may surprise you that I don't have strong views on covering letters and emails, other than if you are asked for one then compose the best one you possibly can. Remember to check that the terminology coincides with that used by the business. It may sound obvious, but this is often where the 'cut and paste' option kicks in and seems to have a mind of its own (that's polite code for 'silly mistakes are easily made'). Ensure it provides what's been requested.

There are some obvious points here around etiquette and good sense. It's a good idea to signpost your audience; consider using subheadings to emphasise your points. Be clear on your audience and resist the temptation to duplicate all the detail from your CV, in favour of a focused summary of how you match the job/person criteria provided.

Example

> *I am interested in this role because it will make good use of my recent project management qualification. I have listed my project management career highlights below, although my CV provides more detail and context.*
> - *Delivered technology refresh project ahead of schedule realising savings of £500k*
> - *Three years' team leadership and £1.5m annual budget – created a high-performance culture*
> - *Five years' project management experience gained in a regulated environment*
> - *PRINCE 2 qualification (2024)*

Your story, your CV, your pitch

It's probably my most controversial advice yet: I am recommending that if your CV sparkles, it's the only one you'll need. You've told a unique story, threaded it through your CV and now it's your shop window. What's to change – you're you, right? For me, tailoring your communication doesn't mean endless iterations of your CV. If it's not pulling in the crowds and getting you interviews, by all means, review it.

Consider third-party feedback

When a trusted recruiter or headhunter suggests some minor additions, review what you've written and consider their feedback. Then, sleep on it, and make a judgement – will that change or addition better reflect who you are / what you want to say?

Update CVs consciously

I'm basing my best advice on a career spent interviewing candidates for roles at all organisational levels and from a broad range of professions or sectors. It's not my style to embarrass individuals and my memory isn't *that* good, although I've experienced my fair share of uncomfortable COOs and CFOs who've forgotten what they did as 'acting' CEO. Was this a real experience (I ask myself) or something someone suggested might help their case, so they added it to their CV hurriedly … then forgot?

When technology gets in the way

Then there are the diligent managers who are embarrassed that I've been working from an out-of-date CV (submitted by a third party). Most candidates want to impress, although too many or too frequent CV updates can lead to confusion. Make it easy for yourself, don't tinker with your CV to please a recruiter, unless you keep incredibly detailed notes or have a good memory!

Consistency

* Person (you)
* Story (yours)
* CV
* Socials theme
* Pitch (yours)

In case you're in any doubt

Sometimes it's worth revisiting your story in the light of feedback received, especially common themes, just to make sure that it's appealing to as broad an audience as is practical. Also, that your messaging is being received as you intended. Let's make it strong as well as consistent.

Top tip – Remember to balance any need to tailor your communications with what you believe to be your key or unique selling points

Chapter Nine

Research employers who show interest

"If you spot an opportunity and are really excited by it,
throw yourself into it with everything you've got."

Richard Branson, Virgin group

Introduction

Most of us know that research is an essential element of recruitment because everyone tells us to do it, don't they? I'm not going to focus on how to do it here, rather provide insight into what research is most likely to help you. When to do it and what to research are keys to your success. I appreciate that you won't want to waste valuable time on too many red herrings, although it's good to be prepared. When a recruiter makes contact or you see an opportunity that interests you, then that's the time to at least do a quick online search. The search will help you to frame some questions for the recruiter or prepare you for creating a great application.

The process

Try to assemble a clear picture of the likely recruitment process early on. Recruiters will want to help you, although they are sometimes left out of the communication loop by their clients. Likewise, some friends want to help with their experiences, only to find that in their geography it's a totally different activity. When faced with these anomalies, it's well worth doing all you can to validate what you've heard, while keeping the recruiter on side.

Ask the right questions

I've devoted a chapter of this guide to your interview questions (Chapter Twelve, page 74) although I wanted to touch on questions here. Asking the right questions will help you to gather the right information and satisfy your research objectives. You may find it helpful to jot down any nagging doubts or questions raised during your research, so that if you're invited to interview, you'll be better prepared.

The organisation

Try not to be drawn in by any prior knowledge that you have about the organisation, particularly when that knowledge may be out of date. A classic example of this could be your out-of-date knowledge of some of the well-known energy companies previously known for fossil fuels, e.g., BP. "Our purpose is reimagining energy for people and our planet. We want to help the world reach net zero and improve people's lives" is BP's more recent aspiration.

Organisation values

What are the organisation's values and to what extent do they match your expectations? And to what extent do these values permeate the fabric of the organisation? If the organisation is open to visitors, e.g., retail and hospitality venues, a public building or space, it's easy to assess this for yourself by visiting and asking questions.

Market forces

What's been in the news recently that has or will have an impact on the organisation? What have been the recent or anticipated changes in the sector, e.g., well-established brands leaving the high street and moving to an online-only distribution model. Researching the sector, what's happening? Focus on key competitors, market share and challenger brands. When considering the public sector, which services are under significant pressure, and which will need to expand?

Ask the recruiter

I haven't met a recruiter (internal or third party) or a headhunter who doesn't want to help their clients seek out and appoint talented individuals to join them. From time to time, I've come across businesses that aren't great at briefing their suppliers (internal or third party) and providing them with sufficient detail. And I've collaborated with some great suppliers who occasionally feel the need to fill in some of the gaps. Most times, they get it right (based on what they know), and other times, they're a bit off beam. On balance, I'm urging you to put your trust in the recruiters and work with them, rather than going it alone.

Get to know the people who matter

Depending on your business experience, you'll not appreciate my describing in detail how to do this or cautioning on confidentiality. It's important to include interviewers, business leaders and other key stakeholders, as well as potential colleagues. Perhaps there are some obvious links to your existing networks? There's nothing quite like making your own judgement based on what you experience first-hand, although it's always useful to learn about personalities and reputation from those whom you trust.

Trust your instincts

I'm encouraging you to keep an open mind for as long as possible, so that you gather as much information as you possibly can, before drawing conclusions about the organisation and its people. There will be times when heritage stories about the business or its personalities are simply that and it's time for change. It could be that the people with the less than acceptable reputation are the people who are leaving the business. I'm encouraging you to trust your instincts, based on what information you collect and the reliability of its source. Remember, the only time you will need to make a final decision about whether or not to accept an offer is once the offer is made to you. Try not to deselect from the process too soon.

Chapter Ten

Prepare for interviews (always)

Sometimes it's easier said than done, especially when you're not entirely sure what to expect from the interview. I'd love to say that you'll get all the information you need in advance, although that's not always the case. The informal interview you'd anticipated becomes an interrogation and, sometimes, it's so informal you may wonder what all the fuss was about.

I've used this chapter to explore interviews, as well as some other activities that may be included – auditions, presentations and more.

The essential ingredients

The good news is that, as you've worked through Chapters One to Three, you'll have refreshed your strengths and achievements, as well as revitalising your story. This is all part of your interview preparation. If you've read the previous chapter (Nine), then you've already put more of the building blocks in place with your research. Other essential elements of preparation are:

- Practising out loud your answers to potential questions, Chapter Eleven on page 71
- Being clear on your questions – what you need to know, Chapter Twelve on page 74

It's a two–way process

A successful interview should resemble a purposeful conversation, rather than an unstructured chat or an interrogation. It's about giving and receiving information. Ideally, the employer gives information about the organisation and the role, then asks questions to better understand the candidate's fit. While this is going on, the candidate gets to know more about the role and the organisation, as well as asking their own questions. If only more interviewers took that on board, they'd get so much more from their candidates.

I want to help you to be a well-prepared candidate, even if your interviewer isn't up to it on the day. I want you to be prepared for all kinds of different interviews – formal or informal, excellent or shabby, tough or a walk in the park.

Questions

It's important that I don't overwhelm you with HR jargon or unnecessary detail, although some employers and recruiters love their exclusive language or their labels, e.g., competency-based interview, biographical interview. Some employers provide questions in advance to aid understanding. Most interviews comprise questions that are designed to find out about:

- **Your motivations for work and the role** – often referred to as motivational questions
- **How you make decisions at work** – often referred to as situational judgement questions
- **How you relate to others** – leadership, teamworking, customer service and so on
- **Your greatest achievements** – at work, in education and in life more generally
- **Your technical expertise** – sometimes referred to as your professional skills

Different types of interview
 • Unstructured – "tell me about yourself" • Competency-based – you are invited to answer questions with real examples • Technical – focus on your vocational know-how • Behavioural event – you are invited to share examples of recent achievements • Biographical – focus on education / career development / what you've done / when and how you've progressed • Structured – tell me about your work / motivations or situational judgement

Example interview questions
,,   • All different styles – some better than others • The best questions provide you with opportunities to demonstrate suitability • Open questions, e.g. tell us about / what is your greatest achievement? • Closed questions, e.g. do you prefer sparkling or still water? • Try to avoid a single word answer to a closed question, "I prefer sparkling water, it's more refreshing" • Use as many real examples as you can remember to demonstrate suitability • Questions aren't (typically) designed to catch you out

Top tip – If you get interview questions in advance, remember the interview is not a memory test.

It's all coming together

It's a good idea to gather as much information as you can about what to expect, e.g., what are the competencies (behaviours or capabilities) to be evaluated. I'm hoping that you are in good shape to answer questions about your strengths and greatest achievements from Chapter One. After that, my best advice is to begin with understanding your motivations at work in a little more detail and what appeals most about the organisation.

There are some example questions for you to be getting on with on the next page and I'm sure you'll have others. Once you've mastered your answers to motivational questions, it's a good idea to think about how you interact with others (whether that's team colleagues or customers). Are you the collaborator, the motivator or the innovator?

Top tip – Remember to practise answering questions with the organisation and the opportunity in mind, rather than a focus on what's not worked elsewhere.

Potential questions

Example motivational questions
 • What does motivation mean to you? • What motivates you at work / at home? • What do you enjoy most at work? • How do you know you're doing a good job? • What motivates you about delivering excellent customer service? • What excites you about this role? • What made you apply for this role?

Remember to prepare potential answers to questions based on the organisation's values, what you know about the business strategy or the five-year business plan as well as any other topic areas you're briefed on. I'm not suggesting that you learn your answers by rote, just that you have some strong examples to hand that will help to demonstrate your suitability.

Some organisations may provide you with example questions to demonstrate their unique culture. Also, it's becoming popular to provide questions in advance to help those candidates who need a little more consideration or time to understand what's required. When you've prepared your 'ideal' answers, remember to practise them out loud. There's more about this technique in Chapter Eleven on page 71.

Example relationship-building questions
 • What is your preferred style when working with others? • How have you built relationships with team colleagues? • What is your preferred leadership role – the coach, the motivator, the trusted adviser, the trailblazer? • How have you got clients on board with your ideas? • What is your preferred influencing style?

A few things to consider when preparing for a virtual interview

Introduction

Video has become an essential element of virtual recruitment processes. Fingers crossed, the organisation that invites you to interview will provide all the information you need to make it a success, including whether they are recording the meeting. Some may even provide a briefing note, FAQs or hints and tips, although here are a few ideas to get your started.

Key contacts

Know who to contact (and how) when the call doesn't seem to be happening as planned or there's an apparent loss of signal or some other technical challenge.

Signal strength

Whichever provider is selected for the meeting, success is entirely dependent on (1) wi-fi and wi-fi signal strength in both locations (yours and theirs) or (2) your mobile network coverage. Check both.

Technical challenges

Sometimes insufficient bandwidth causes poor picture quality or sound disruption/distortion, so try to find a location with a strong signal. Get comfortable with the technology. Check sound, camera and lighting, so that there are no surprises on the day of the interview.

Location

Once you've identified the best camera-ready space, it's important that you are comfortable in your space. Aim for a chair that creates a strong posture (rather than a chaise longue) and if you're unsure, it's worth a quick test video to check camera height. This will also highlight any unnecessary distractions from piles of untidy papers, discarded clothes or flickering lights.

Practise makes perfect

Unless you are a seasoned performer, it's a good idea to practise looking at the camera, engaging your audience and creating impact. It may be helpful to check out a short recording of yourself to troubleshoot.

Dress to impress

Take your lead from the organisational style (as you would with any interview), although some bright colours, bold patterns and stripes aren't always great on video, particularly if they clash with your curtains.

Interruptions

There may be a time during the interview when the unexpected happens and the doorbell rings, the dog barks or someone bursts into the room uninvited. Recognise that life happens and try not to let it disrupt your cool unnecessarily.

Answering questions, sharing stories and asking questions

You want to contribute fully to the discussion, although sometimes it's more difficult to spot when someone is about to speak on video – try not to speak over other participants or stay quiet unnaturally.

Top tip – Remember to prepare your camera-ready space and test the technology, so that you begin your interview on a positive note.

On camera

Join the workshop 'in person' with your camera and microphone switched on, although, of course, it's helpful if background noise is minimal and you're in an environment that you feel happy to share on camera.

Q&A

You may find it helpful to list the questions you hope will be answered and even find that ticking them off as they are answered will help you to get the most benefit from the Q&A session at the end of the interview. Virtual interviews are more likely to run to exact time slots, as there's no comfortable reception for the next candidate to experience.

Auditions, presentations and more

I've decided to begin with "A" for assessment centre, although first there are some general points that should help with confidence on the day. I've been looking forward to writing this chapter, although now the time has come, I'm in a quandary. There's so much I could write about to demonstrate my own knowledge, although that's not always helpful to you. So, I'm hoping that I've got the balance right here, without scaring you off.

First things first

I've frequently supported candidates who wish they'd better understood what was required. Some hadn't read the instructions provided in sufficient detail, while others didn't quite grasp what was required of them. Here are my top tips for success. Occasionally, I hear that candidates weren't briefed on what to expect on the day. My best advice to you all is: do your research and ask questions for clarity.

1. Once you know what's required of you, it's likely that you'll receive comprehensive notes from the employer about what to expect on the day.
2. While virtual interviews are relatively trouble-free, some activities and practical skills tests may be a little more challenging. Be clear about what's expected.
3. It may seem obvious today, although when the time comes to prepare your pitch,

remember to read and follow instructions. Timing is often critical.

4. It's a good idea to follow up on any points that aren't clear well in advance and try not to leave anything to chance on the day.

5. Some elements give you greater flexibility, offering opportunities for interpretation and influence over outcomes, e.g., presentations, rather than requiring the right answer to a specific question.

6. Try to put time aside for preparation in advance where it's necessary or recommended – as with all challenges, preparation will help to improve your performance on the day.

7. Sometimes several different elements are combined, e.g., you may be invited to consider a case study, then prepare and deliver a presentation based around the case study and your answers.

8. Remember to articulate your assumptions at the beginning of a project, explanation or presentation, e.g., for the purpose of this exercise, I've assumed a budget of £x is available.

Assessment centre

Not a place but an assortment of carefully selected activities for individual and group execution. It is most likely that you'll receive an overview in advance, although precise details of each exercise will be provided on the day. Individual interviews and activities are likely, although presentations may require a team effort. My best advice is to practise any activities you know may or will be included and remember to support others on the day, as well as making sure that you shine.

Audition

An audition is most likely associated with the arts, e.g., actor, dancer, musician, performer, entertainer, presenter, news reporter and so on. The audition may include a set piece, improvisation (around a theme) or the candidate's choice. I was also tempted to include the work of a chef and a florist here because, in many ways, the requirements could be similar in terms of theatre, although I've also covered this on the next page! Remember to practise out loud, be clear on what's required and timings.

Case study

You'll most likely be provided with a scenario and invited to comment or find a solution. There are two or three different approaches and, no surprises, you'll either be invited to (1) bone up in advance of your interview and present your observations or a solution at your interview – there may be a written element to this, or (2) complete the entire exercise on the day of your interview. Remember to check timings as well as the parameters (level of detail) of what's required. It is most likely to be a frequently occurring challenge experienced by the profession or the job role.

Creative or artistic task

This activity has many of the characteristics of an audition and, in some ways, it's down to descriptive words and context, rather than content. It's most likely to be a timed activity (which may include off-site preparation) with a specific creative objective or outcome – something you'd frequently encounter in the role, e.g., design a logo for a new premium, plant-based food brand. I've included journalism, baking, photography, floristry, design (from fashion through to packaging and everything in between) as well as all things mechanical. Just remember to follow the instructions and you'll do a great job.

Game-based assessments

These hybrid assessments typically measure cognitive ability and seek to assess personality, judgement, numerical skills and risk-taking. Some even assess memory and emotions. Candidates work through a series of interrelated activities. These are accompanied by full instructions and opportunities to practise. Candidates often receive immediate feedback on their performance.

Group task

An opportunity to demonstrate your team skills, e.g., building rapport, communicating, ideas sharing, building consensus and decision making. The task would be shared on the day along with instructions, making it difficult to prepare in advance, other than reminding yourself what great team skills look like. On the day itself, it's a good idea to encourage others to contribute just as much as it is to demonstrate your own strengths.

Stakeholder discussion or round table

This is a variation on the group task introduced above. A discussion topic is usually provided in advance along with the names and roles of other participants. You are invited to prepare questions and participate in the conversation. I encourage you to consider the questions that you may be asked and your likely answers to those questions. Remember to consider the impression you wish to leave with your audience. What would you like them to know about you? What is the story you wish to tell?

Personality profiling and preferences

Different employers favour different tools, although the majority are accompanied by comprehensive instructions and opportunities to practise. In addition to questionnaires designed to highlight your preferences at work, e.g., whether you prefer to work collaboratively or independently, there are questionnaires to determine your motivation preferences and your idea of customer focus. You are invited to rate statements according to the strength of your preference, e.g., agree or strongly agree or select the statement that most and least aligns with your view from a selection of statements.

Practical task

Sometimes referred to as work sampling and, like creative or artistic tasks, they are timed activities that simulate day-to-day work, e.g., making a call to a customer about a late delivery or creating a project plan from a list of different activities. While it's likely that the call would be observed throughout (maybe roleplayed), the project plan would be evaluated upon completion. **Be yourself and hold your nerve – you'll be great.**

Presentation

Presentation questions are frequently set and submitted to candidates in advance of their interview with the expectation that you will attend your interview ready to present your ideas. The practice of inviting candidates to prepare their presentation on the day is less popular right now, with more assessments going online. Perhaps with one notable exception – the group presentation as part of an assessment centre. There's more on presentations on page 69.

Psychometric tests

Measures of intelligence, personality, aptitude and ability may be included in recruitment and good professional practice suggests that candidates (1) are briefed on what to expect and (2) complete practice test examples like those published by SHL Practice Tests and Assessments (SHL: https://www.shl.com/shldirect/en/practice-tests/).

Role play

The exact brief would most likely be given to candidates on the day of the interview, although they would be briefed that a role play on a job-related activity would be included. Candidates may be invited to prepare for and deliver a conversation with a team member who is under-performing or a client who is displeased that a project appears behind schedule.

Site visit

I was in two minds about whether to include site visits in this chapter. These are included to help candidates gain greater insight into the organisation's culture, its people and the working environment. This may help with decision making, but I advise caution and recommend some preparation. It may sound cynical, although if it's part of a selection process, you can still be deselected.

Situational judgement

It's time to assess the judgement required for solving typical work-related challenges and determine the likely behaviours you would demonstrate (how you will or may behave) in each situation. You are presented with hypothetical scenarios (written words or a video clip) – what would you do? You may be presented with several possible options or invited to write in free text. The effectiveness of your potential response is evaluated. You may be asked what led you to the solution.

Skills tests

Put simply, this is a test of your skills in a particular situation and could be as simple as requiring an electrician to begin with wiring a plug. At the more advanced level, this would include a teacher planning a lesson and delivering it to a student audience. Another example may be to invite a pastry chef to create a glazed fruit tart. In all three examples, there would be a time target, although the level of detail provided in advance may vary. The task may be set and communicated in advance or on the day itself.

Technical test or Q&A

A technical skills test is frequently used to assess technical (or vocational) knowledge. It may take the form of a written test, or interviewers may invite candidates to talk through their responses to potential scenarios or specific questions. This approach may be used in professional interviews, e.g., employment legislation (HR) or signal sequencing (signal engineer).

Testing

No surprises here – there are right and wrong answers. There are numerous types of questions and different ways of asking them, e.g., perhaps you are asked to provide the answer or select the answer from a list of potential answers (multiple choice). Accuracy as well as speed will be assessed, so try to answer any practice questions to a timeline.

Video clip

You'll know what a video clip is, I know, although I want you to be prepared to film yourself answering questions (often set by the hiring manager) and uploading the film of your answers via the organisation's recruitment system. The best advice is that you practise answering some questions and filming yourself before you work on the preset questions. It's likely that you'll get an opportunity to upload the best of two or three attempts.

Work-based presentation

This is your opportunity to demonstrate your communication skills and, in particular, your practical presentation skills, not to mention how you tackle a work-based challenge (planning and problem solving) or how you assimilate knowledge and learn.

It's worth remembering that your audience will be assessing your skills as well as your knowledge, so that's delivery as well as content. And, in this instance, delivery is as much about how you articulate your message on the day, as it is about the slides you design to describe your approach or solution. There are likely to be a few additional challenges to navigate, depending on whether you're presenting to a virtual audience or you're all in the same room.

Most organisations provide timings and topic parameters in advance, and the majority set a specific question (or scenario) to be answered (addressed) by the presentation. I've met candidates who've been asked to present for twenty or thirty minutes on how they meet the brief and others who've been invited to present for up to ten minutes on their strategic vision for *xyz*. Both come with their individual challenges: thirty minutes at second stage can feel like duplication of your CV and what you demonstrated at first stage, whereas ten minutes on the next five years may feel like you've been short-changed.

I've collaborated with employers who love slides that mirror their brand identity yet get sniffy when the logo is used in the wrong position on the slide, or the shading is incorrect. And I've worked with others who've commented that they want to see more of the candidate's personality coming through. I usually recommend creating your own brand interpretation with a nod to the employer. There are endless design options available online, although if you're not particularly artistic, keep it simple and relevant.

A few points to remember when preparing and delivering your pitch:

- **Stay true to what you know** already about presenting your ideas
- Be sure to **focus on the task** set
- Remember: **I**ntroduction **N**eed **T**ime **R**ange **O**bjectives
- **Introduce** yourself, your topic (challenge or question) and any assumptions you've made
- Bring out your personality, attitude and your strengths – **it's your presentation**
- Keep slides **relevant, concise and uncluttered** – use images / animation appropriately
- Include **video** or **animation** only where it adds impact and it's relevant
- Master the graphics but **try not to get carried away**
- **Tell a story** – introduce it, tell it and conclude it
- Ensure that **every slide earns its place** in the presentation
- Be sure to **present your ideas** on the day – the slides provide context only
- Include **next steps** (where they're appropriate)
- Invite questions and **get the conversation going** (remember what you practised)
- Be mindful of **timings** – try not to rush or overrun

> **Top tip** – Remember to be clear about what's expected of you – check instructions and timings. Rehearse what you can and prepare for a successful performance.

Chapter Eleven

Practise out loud

All great performances begin with rehearsals. In the same way that actors, musicians and dancers all benefit from practising their routines, it's a good idea to practise your answers to likely interview questions, as well as any presentations you'll need to make. Our performers aren't just practising their moves or timing how long a sequence takes, but how easy it is to change out of one costume and into another. They're seeking to iron out any creases in their delivery, their timings or their overall performance and they're keen to evaluate their impact on their audience.

Connect with your audience

When it comes to practising out loud, I sound like a scratched record, but I make no apology. It's such a worthwhile exercise. I recall phoning a client six months ago to wish them well with their interview only to find them ironing their shirt in readiness for the meeting. And yes, you've guessed it, they were practising out loud at the same time. So, try not to tell yourself that there isn't time! But please remember, practice doesn't mean learning off by heart. An interview is not a recital, and your interviewers need to find a connection with what you have to say. Likewise, presentations need to resonate with your audience. They need to connect with your aspirations and passion to be part of their gig.

Your show, your rehearsal

All too frequently, our stories or our answers to questions seem well-rehearsed and acceptable in our heads, although when we come to speak, they don't sound so great. Sometimes that's because the explanations are overly long, or we don't get to the point of our answer quickly enough. In both instances, we've lost our audience. Full sentences aren't always required. Once you're clear on your story and you've used it to write up your CV, etc., it should be easier to recount. A little practice is never wasted, so I recommend that you begin with your profile (elevator not required), then move on to some questions.

Critical evaluation

Interview questions vary enormously, although motivational questions (in all different guises) are inevitable and a good place to go next. You may find it helpful to record/film your answers to questions, then review them for fluency and impact. It's even better if you can find someone who's willing to ask the questions and review your answers with you. Audience feedback is priceless, especially presentation feedback. If your enthusiasm begins to wane, it's worth remembering that you may even get an interview question about how you prepare for important events.

A critical reminder of the inevitable example motivational questions
<ul><li>What does motivation mean to you?</li><li>What motivates you at work / at home?</li><li>What do you enjoy most at work?</li><li>How do you know you're doing a good job?</li><li>What motivates you about delivering excellent customer service?</li><li>What excites you about this role?</li><li>What made you apply for this role?</li></ul>

Over to you

Remember to include the questions you're likely to find more challenging to answer. Try to cover the broad range, including technical questions where they are relevant. After all, practice makes perfect, and all great performances need a dress rehearsal. **Good luck!**

Chapter Twelve

Be clear on your questions
(what you need to know)

Introduction

I'm encouraging you to compile a list of what you need to know about the opportunity, team colleagues, key stakeholders, employment terms and the organisation (values, strategy, business plan), as the recruitment process plays out. And, of course, you'll need to find out about the recruitment process itself early on. Some aspects will be more important to you than others and your priorities may vary according to where you are with your career, personal development and qualification. Your occupation will also have a bearing on your priority areas.

Some ideas to get you started

I've provided some space for your jottings at the end of the chapter (page 77) and suggested a few headings you might want to consider here, although I'm sure you'll come up with lots more:
- About the **recruitment** process – different stages and priorities
- About **timelines** – recruitment milestones and start date, etc.
- About the **role**, its **objectives** and **current projects**
- About **budgets**
- About your **team** – how many, where, etc.
- About **personal development** and learning opportunities
- About essential **qualifications**, sponsorship
- About the prevailing **management style** (your manager, etc.)
- About the **organisation** and significant projects

- About the organisation **values**/culture
- About employment – locations and expectations, **employment terms**, etc.
- About **next steps**
- About **your induction**/orientation
- About internal progress, sponsored **training**/qualification and promotion

Open questions

Remember to ask open questions that require a full and informative answer, rather than ones that require a simple, one-word answer. After all, you want to keep the conversation going. There's more information about different question styles on pages 58 and 59, although it's written from the interviewer's perspective.

Straight from the horse's mouth

I'm sure that if you are collaborating with a third-party recruiter or headhunter, they'll provide background information about many of the above topics. It's likely that answers will come from different sources, although there'll be some questions you'll *only* want the hiring manager to answer. I'm sure that you will want to hear about their preferred style and what's important to them. I recommend asking these questions for yourself at interview, rather than hearing answers second or third hand. But that doesn't mean you can't seek reinforcement.

Be prepared

All great interviews usually conclude with a Q&A session (this may be cut short or rushed if it's a virtual interview and the next meeting is imminent). I'm certain that you'll have been asked before, "What questions do you have for us?" and you've frozen, so it's important to feel prepared. Remember, it's your time to demonstrate (through your questions) that you've thought about the opportunity. It's so much easier to come up with questions and jot them down as you think of them, then cross them off as they're answered (outside of the interview).

Try not to waffle

It can feel awkward when all your questions seem to have been answered during an interview. If this happens to you, then try to resist the opportunity to ask a weak question just for the sake of it. It may be more helpful to ask even more about a topic that interests you:

- "Could you please tell me a little more about *xyz*?"
- "Could you please tell me more about my first thirty days?"
- "I'd like to hear more about how the team communicates while working remotely."
- "How long have you worked here and what do you love most about it?"

Questions	Notes

🖉 **Remember you can write any outstanding points (after your interview) here for future reference**

_____

_____

_____

_____

_____

_____

Chapter Thirteen

Accept a role because it works for you and you'll flourish

Power of influence

Where are you most likely to flourish? It's tough when you're in a role that doesn't work for you. Maybe that's because the business's values aren't in line with yours, or perhaps you love the corporate ethos but not the organisation structure and the work you're signed up to deliver. It may be challenging, although with vision and the magical gift of influence, you *can* make change happen. But changing business values (when it's not your business) can be energy sapping. That's why I'm encouraging you to carefully consider your options and expectations.

Getting ahead

Just as the best time to compile your CV is when you don't need it, now I'm encouraging you to list what's important to you before you need it. You've already devoted some time to thinking about your values (Chapter One) and now it's time to dig a bit deeper. Consider the topics most likely to help you decide whether an organisation and/or a particular opportunity is/are right for you. It's so much easier to do this when your future is not depending on it, and you don't need to think about the disadvantages. That comes later once you've been offered the opportunity. I've included the beginnings of a worked example on page 80 to demonstrate the approach. I hope that the example will get you started, although I'm sure you'll come up with your own list.

Listen to those nagging doubts

Sometimes it's easier to reject an offer when you're already working than it is when you're not. In times of high unemployment, any offer may appear attractive, so I'm encouraging you to listen to those nagging voices inside your head. If it's the voice that is reminding you of the haphazard recruitment process, the dictatorial leadership style on show or the apparent lack of business ethics, then please listen, or at least grab a little more time to work through the details.

Work through the detail of any offer

Make yourself a cuppa, grab something to write with (or type on) and evaluate the opportunity. For example, if the role is offered on a part-time basis, how do the working hours fit with your other ideas for a portfolio career? If the role isn't at the organisational level you aspire to, how could you balance that?

More disadvantages than advantages

This is not going to be an easy decision to make, although I suspect you know that already, especially if you're not currently in full-time employment and you need to be. Now may be the right time to double-check your reasoning and revisit the risks. Then, when you're certain that your success criteria are spot on, consider whether a further chat with the recruiter or the hiring manager may help to allay your concerns. You'll know how much (or how little) to share with key stakeholders based on the relationships you've forged.

> **Top tip** – Remember if you've got any doubts about the opportunity on offer, it's not too late to ask additional questions.

Topic	Advantages	Disadvantages
Location – working from home, with three days per month office	No need to relocate as office days will be infrequent	Finding a regular inspirational, yet quiet space to work
Working hours		
Job content		
Job level		
Organisation		
Organisation values		
Management style		
Terms and conditions of employment		

Saying thanks, but no thanks

Facing up to your worst fears and standing by your decision can be daunting, although it can be liberating as well as confidence boosting. It's worth remembering that the organisation will have invested time in reaching the decision to hire you, but if it hasn't impressed you sufficiently, then that's unlikely to change overnight. It's a good idea to be prompt and polite with your communication, should you find yourself in this predicament and give your reasons succinctly. Try not to drag this out unnecessarily or, worse still, ghost the recruiter or the potential employer.

Even if the organisation or the role didn't impress you, you may come across the stakeholders again in a different organisational context. Or you may be interested in a different role in the same organisation. Remember the headhunters and the third-party recruiters, especially the ones who impressed. Plan to keep those conversations flowing.

What to do when recruitment progress resembles buses

Working through the advantages and disadvantages of an opportunity systematically can seem like a bit of a chore, although it's also the best way to compare several offers (should they come along at the same time). Especially if the jobs and/or the organisations are quite different. And if you're finding it difficult to go it alone, why not enlist the help of a friend or someone from your network? Here are a few worked examples to get you started.

Topic	Organisation 1	Organisation 2
Location	Working from home mostly, only three days per month office-based	Primarily office-based with flexibility as priorities dictate
Working hours	Contracted hours forty per week, with occasional weekend working	Some unsociable shifts, although contracted hours thirty-five per week
Values – mine and theirs	Social conscience, anti-slavery, D&I at every opportunity	Relaxed, 'go-ahead', pioneers of change, inclusivity obvious

Buy a bit of time

I'm often asked by candidates how they can buy some time during the recruitment process. Perhaps the timeline for the ideal or favourite opportunity is (or appears to be) progressing more slowly than the second-placed opportunity. In a difficult jobs market, then my advice tends to focus on keeping all your options open for as long as possible. In other words, back both horses each way. Stick with the process until it concludes, and the offers come in. That's the only time you'll need to compare options and make decisions – try not to meet trouble halfway.

Quick, quick, slow

It's a kind of balancing act. Aim to keep as many stakeholders updated as need to be, fiercely protect your reputation as a serious player, and work relentlessly to make the best decision for you at this time. Easily said, I know, although try not to be pushed around. I know how influential headhunters and recruiters can be (I've been one), so it's time to practise your great negotiation skills. Remember, if you've got any doubts about the opportunity on offer, it's not too late to ask additional questions. Most employers would prefer to learn that you are taking them seriously, rather than turning them down.

The final countdown

Now you've made your lists and hopefully they've helped you to reach your decision about the offer(s) you've received. But just before you sign the contract, remember to ask yourself one more time: "Will the role work for me and how will I flourish?" Then listen to your answer:

- **A hesitation or a 'no'** – refresh your memory – what's important to you?
- **A resounding 'yes'** – you've cracked it, well done and now it's time to own your own future

Own your own future

Now that you've accepted an offer, why not jot down your short to medium-term objectives as you think of them? Perhaps you already had some personal development objectives in mind before you achieved this success, or maybe the recruitment process has highlighted some development opportunities for you to explore. Either way, they're all relevant to your continued success.

Explanation

The SMART acronym is widely used across many organisations with a few variations, so it's a good place to begin. Once you have a clearer idea of your deliverables in the new role, it'll be easy to update what you've created to fit with the organisation's performance approach.

S is for Specific	Although you might have an aspiration to 'Get better at project management', this is too broad ... which aspects need improvement?
M is for Measurable	Identify how something will change and how you will measure that change, e.g., a 1% increase in margin
A is for Achievable	You may have high hopes, although it's important that you are set up for success
R is for Realistic	Be clear on what you can realistically achieve in the time limit – dream big, but not too big ...
T is for Time-based	Be clear and realistic on how long it will take to achieve your goals or how long you've got, e.g., a 1% increase in margin month on month for one year

My new role, my objectives

	What's next for me? What do I aspire to achieve?
1	
2	
3	
4	
5	

Feedback success stories

I applaud the organisations that take the time to offer objective and meaningful feedback to candidates like you, who engage in their recruitment processes. For me, that means feedback that candidates (like you) can use to improve their performance or contribution next time around. Most successful candidates pick up some insights or feedback on their contribution from headhunters and recruiters, as well as from their own progress through the different stages of assessment. More detailed feedback for successful candidates is often overlooked, although it can really help you to understand the new environment. I'm encouraging you to ask.

Colour and contrast

I'm a big fan of detailed feedback for *successful* candidates (like you). My reasons are easily explained. I've participated in so many candidate review sessions that really bring colour and contrast to a candidate's performance. Although the discussion contributes to the decision making and the eventual outcome of the process (to hire), it's not always shared beyond the reviewing managers.

If you believe that this constructive colour and contrast will benefit your future success, then please pursue it. Sometimes it's all too easy to celebrate the success of a new role and forget what got you there. Wouldn't you rather know that your presentation was on message and delivered with style, although a little too detailed? Especially if that feedback will help you to succeed in the new role.

There's some space below for you to jot down a few notes about (1) what you've learned about yourself and (2) what you've heard that might help now that you've secured a new role.

What I've learned about myself during this job search

Recruitment progress

It's a good idea to review your progress throughout the entire job search / recruitment process – what went particularly well and what went less well? What have you learned about yourself? What might you do differently next time and what will you repeat because it was such a success? Then, when the time comes to write the next chapter of your story and update your CV, consider how far you've come since you first picked up a copy of this guide.

Celebrate your successes and achievements. Try to remember that recruitment isn't a breeze and starting a new job can be just as challenging. You're not on your own, there are always people around who will be pleased to help you. That applies whether you're the new CEO or it's your first role after full-time education. And one final point from me: remember to extend your network to include all those new people who've impressed you throughout your journey.

What I need to follow up or remember

Write their contact details here

Extending my network

Chapter Fourteen

Recruitment, it's not an easy ride

It's long been my ambition to keep people positive and encourage them not to dwell on the difficulties or challenges of recruitment. My preference has been to focus on supporting jobseekers to be the best that they can be. Acknowledging some of the early feedback on this text (guide), I've included this short piece on just how tough job hunting can be.

I recognise that, when you are not working, a few days or a week can feel like an eternity. Remember to make a plan to fill your days with a balance of job seeking and other activities – if there aren't any more recruitment tasks on your to-do list today then try something else.

When the going gets tough

Deadlines and turnaround times are often unrealistic, although candidates are expected to be committed to the task of getting their CVs and cover letters to recruiters at speed. Much earlier in this book, I wrote about the benefits of always having an up-to-date, good quality CV ready to circulate. This eases some of the pain of not having sufficient time to do what's required when you see an advert for your ideal role or hear about a great employer from the recruiter.

From time to time, closing dates appear in adverts and are withdrawn without warning. That's when you as the candidate assume the job has been filled, although you don't necessarily hear that from the recruiters. All in all, it can feel a bit like taking a chance on the lottery. Should I apply anyway or not? My advice is to communicate rather than to assume, especially when you have contact names of recruiters.

You're expected to be committed and current (up to date with what's going on around you), although recruitment deadlines and turnaround times are often unrealistic. You put in the effort and then, silence. No promised call-backs, no updates and no feedback. Remember that you are not alone; if you've not heard, it's likely that other candidates haven't been updated either.

My best advice is to seek feedback on process outcomes, especially if you've invested your time in attending interviews. Follow up (at least once), although if only to demonstrate your commitment and satisfy yourself that you tried. It's a difficult time – you agonise over feelings of disappointment, expectation and irritation. That's perfectly normal, although try to stay upbeat. You're not on your own.

Sharing the love

Drawing on my HR expertise and resourcing specialism, I've amassed a wealth of recruitment knowledge that I'm happy to share with you. I've always taken the view that expertise once shared leaves space in my head for more learning. I mention this here as creating this guide is my way of sharing the love when I need a diversion from some of the other challenges of everyday life. Maybe you're a writer in the making?

Absence of courtesy

Recruitment is a business process that most often begins with a need to fill a vacant (or soon to be vacant) role. After that, the workflow is easily determined, whatever the type of organisation, its size or the sector. Much of the process is automated or driven by technology and powered by AI, although, for me, recruitment is still about finding a great person to do an excellent job for a fabulous organisation. That doesn't need endless interviews and extended timelines, let alone an absence of courtesy and polite communications. Right now, I get that you may be caught up in that time warp. If you are, it's all about being kind to yourself and staying positive.

Mastering the fundamentals

Recruitment means different things to different people, although we owe it to ourselves to recognise and master the fundamentals. That includes mastering some ways to counteract the challenges and disappointments. It's easy for me to suggest keeping your frustrations at bay but how? Take a look at some of the ideas below and see if any resonate with you. **Have fun!**

Things to try:
· Walk in the countryside or by the sea
· Salsa outdoors in the sunshine or dance around the house
· Sing like there's nobody listening
· Write a list of 'good ideas' to try or new people to contact
· Think outside the box – how could you use your strengths differently?
· Consider whether there are new specialisms you should be exploring
· Volunteering – who might benefit from your skills?
· Begin a new hobby or pastime, or take an existing one to the next level
· Recognise that you're on a roller coaster with high and low points
· Satisfy yourself that your networking is right up to date

Sounds easy, I know, although most of us recognise the volume of personal effort that goes into securing a brilliant and fulfilling role. Effort which sometimes dwindles along with enthusiasm over time. And if that's not disheartening enough, there's the added challenge of unemployment. This is not the right place to get stuck into the complexities of the labour market or the influence of inflation (rising costs of living) on opportunities. Job hunting is tough, and the market can be unwelcoming, as well as unpredictable.

I'm all for keeping people positive, especially when the going gets tough, although our journey together won't always be easy. Right now, recruitment is not for the fainthearted; it takes guts and determination. There will be disappointments, and you will experience lapses of confidence, but remember to focus on the things you can control or do differently next time. And remember to ask for help before you need it. This is your time to be the star of your own show. Imagine how you'll feel once you secure a new role or restart your career. There's a job out there with your name on it, we just need to work together to find it.

I've long argued that recruitment concludes once a person is settled and performing well in their new role. In other words, at the end of their introduction to the organisation and once they've agreed their objectives with their sponsor. But where does recruitment begin? For individuals, it starts with a desire or a need to find a new role, and for organisations, it begins with being the kind of employer people want to join. It does, doesn't it? Perhaps some employers see it differently and still feel recruitment is simply their choice, beginning with a vacancy to get work done. I'll let you decide! Fortunately, in the UK, we have organisations like ACAS and CIPD to advise.

It's worth remembering that as a candidate you should be treated fairly and not disadvantaged during the recruitment process. This applies equally to potential employers or recruitment third parties collaborating with you. Most organisations ensure that their colleagues are well-versed in the legal narrative surrounding recruitment, as well as protected characteristics and good practice. Processes and decision making are monitored to ensure the absence of bias.

From time to time, in your search for a new role, it's likely that you will encounter some good practice, e.g., names removed from your CV or application to avoid any conscious or unconscious bias. That said, less than perfect practices are still prevalent – I don't condone unlawful or substandard practices, and you shouldn't either, although you may find yourself challenged.

It's often the friendly chit chat about home location and travel arrangements, assumptions about home circumstances or the blatant questions (suppositions) about beliefs that may throw you off course. My best recommendation is that, ahead of any recruitment-related conversation, meeting or interview, you are clear on:

- What you are happy to share
- How you might respond to such intrusive questions or comments
- How you will restore balance to the interaction and avoid a silent pause

The Equality Act 2010 Protected characteristics
· Age
· Disability
· Race
· Religion or belief
· Sex (gender)
· Sexual orientation
· Gender reassignment
· Marriage and civil partnership
· Pregnancy and maternity

A more recent term that's crept into our recruitment lexicon is 'ghosting'. I've written about the term elsewhere in this text, although I just want to remind you that it's:

- Appalling practice not to be excused or condoned
- Less about you and more about the bad manners of the other person
- To be discouraged (or called out) at every opportunity (but not to disadvantage you)

In the same way that not every interview will be a great interview, not every recruitment experience will be a positive one. I've prepared you for what might come your way in the name of recruitment. I wanted to ensure that your knowledge and confidence shine through because you're feeling confident about your story and your aspirations. Good luck!

Top tip – Remember to be kind to yourself and try to remain positive. If feedback isn't forthcoming, follow up once then draw a line and jump over it. Don't beat yourself up.

Chapter Fifteen

Our adventure together

When I began writing this guide, I wondered whether I'd find sufficient material of good quality to keep you interested. I was keen to deliver my advice and suggested strategies in an engaging and 'less is more' kind of way – just like a good CV. I wanted you to have fun trying out a few new approaches and challenging yourself to work differently. So, how did I do?

Coming back for more

There's nothing worse than investing in a book, spending time reading it and then wishing you hadn't. Time as well as finances are precious and that's why I wanted to create a text you might become addicted to; something you might even want to recommend to friends. I hope you've found this guide inspirational as well as helpful in your quest to secure your next opportunity.

My aspiration

I dreamed of a well-thumbed guide with doodles and scribbles initially or, if you prefer it, an electronic version that you could bookmark. Either way, I wanted it to mark the start of our journey; a reference book, as well as a journal of your notes, examples as you think of them and what you've learned until they're needed in future.

Your focus

The world of work moves at pace, although any fundamental changes to how organisations want you to apply for their roles is usually well signposted and more gradual, even the impacts of technology on recruitment. I urge you to keep these changes in perspective. It's essential that you understand what's required of you and *most* organisations will provide clear guidance. Focus on *that* before listening to others' interpretations of what you should be doing.

	The foundations of your success
1	Know yourself – your values, aspirations, strengths and achievements
2	Be clear on your story and tell it with confidence (stay positive)
3	Ask for help before you need it and use your networks
4	Keep your CV clear and relevant – avoid repetition and overcrowding
5	Spend as long as you can on research, although if you only have an hour, use it wisely and try not to squander it on negative energy
6	Do what's asked of you – a two-page CV in Word format is just that, resist the temptation to attach a three-page PDF
7	Answer interview questions succinctly – interviewers will usually ask for more detail, although they may not stop you waffling
8	Practise out loud, especially if you've been asked to prepare a presentation
9	Rehearse any additional tasks – whether that's arranging a floral display, filleting a fish or dancing the salsa
10	Only accept a job that's right for you

What's next for you?

Congratulations, we've come a long way together. No doubt there have been a few bumps in the road for you, although I'm hoping that you're still feeling energised. Here's a space to jot down:

- How you'll approach your job search in future
- What you're going to do differently
- Any outstanding questions you need answered

Write your ideas here

_____

_____

_____

_____

_____

_____

_____

_____

_____

_____

_____

_____

_____

_____

_____

We've almost come to the end of our adventure together and it may be that you have more questions or want to discuss a specific topic in a little more detail. My website may help, especially Tea Break — Heather Watt (https://www.heatherwatt.co.uk/tea-break), where you'll find an eclectic mix of stories about recruitment, work and life more generally.

How did I do?

I hope you have found some helpful strategies to aid your success with job hunting and securing a new role. Like most people, feedback is important to me. It helps me to improve the material and products I create. I'd love to hear what you think and how useful this guide has been to you, plus any areas that you'd like to see expanded. You can always use the Let's chat (https://www.heatherwatt.co.uk/lets-chat) facility on my website to contact me.

> If something needs to change or you need a fresh approach, beginning the conversation is the most difficult thing you'll need to do ... let's get networking.

Jargon buster

Jargon
• Jargon is often defined as, "special words or phrases used by some professions or professionals in a particular context." Often to boast exclusivity.
• From time to time, jargon may be necessary to demonstrate your knowledge of a specific topic or to determine a strength related to a critical profession.
• My recommendation is to use jargon sparingly because, without explanation, it may confuse your audience, especially if you are hoping to change career direction.
• Abbreviations can sometimes be misinterpreted, especially if the same abbreviation is used in multiple different contexts.
• Example: Organisation Design and Organisation Development often share the OD abbreviation, although they are distinctly different practices.
• My best advice? Remember to explain your terms (jargon or abbreviations) without exception.

The following provides a little more information about some of the words used in this text and the relevant page number where the word or term first appears.

ACAS   Page 90
- Advisory, Conciliation and Arbitration Service
- Promotes better UK employment relations

Achievements   Page 8
- The positive things that you have done in your life that you are proud of

Artificial Intelligence (AI)
- AI algorithms enable machines (computers) to simulate human intelligence and execute often complex tasks autonomously

Assessment centres
- A collection of tasks, tests and interviews to assess your strengths / capabilities

Candidate
- A job seeker who has shown interest in a role / is going through a recruitment process

CIPD
- Chartered Institute of Personnel and Development
- The professional body for HR and people development, employers and policy makers

CEO (Chief Executive Officer)
- The most senior member of the organisation and possibly the business owner

Competencies
- The things that you do and the behaviours that you demonstrate when working

COO (Chief Operating Officer)
- The most senior member of the team who is accountable for the operation

Credentials
- A qualification, an achievement or an asset that suggests suitability for a role

C-Suite
- Chief Officers of an organisation, e.g. COO Chief Operating Officer, CFO Chief Finance Officer, CPO Chief People Officer, and so on

CV
- An abbreviation for Curriculum Vitae. A catch-all for skills, experience and employment

Entrepreneur
- A brave and curious person who recognises their talent for starting a business

Flourish
- Healthy or vigorous growth and/or development

FOMO (fear of missing out)
- Exactly what it says. Being wary of being left out

Headhunter
- Sometimes known as executive search or research. Third-party adviser

INTRO
You may find it helpful to follow the acronym INTRO to begin your presentation:
- **I**ntroduce yourself and the topic
- **N**eed for the presentation
- **T**ime or duration, plus time for questions
- **R**ange/coverage
- **O**bjectives of the presentation

JD (job description)
- Usually, a written document about your role that describes what's required

Learn
- **Plan** what you're going to do
- **Do** it
- **Review** how it went
- **Revise** how you'd do it next time
- **Repeat**

Networks, networking
- Staying in touch and sharing experiences, as well as learning regularly

Personality
- A unique combination of how you do what you do

Psychometrics and psychometric tests
- Theory and technique of psychological measurement
- A scientific discipline
- Constructing assessment tools to measure (or test) capability and personality

Recruiter
- An in-house or third-party colleague who understands and applies the recruitment process fairly and consistently

Recruitment
- Attracting and securing a suitable person to do a collection of tasks making up a job
- A recognised business process, which is applied fairly and consistently

Reputation
- How a person or an organisation is perceived

Resourcing
- Understanding how work gets done and recommending the best people solution
- This is not always about recruiting a person to do the task

Résumé
- A shorter (1 x page of A4) CV favoured by some cultures

Search
- Targeted research into potential candidate pools
- Seeking candidates who may not even be looking for a new role

Side hustle
- An idea or interest that led to an additional income source (not a primary role)

Situational judgement questions
- Questions that aim to put the respondent in a given situation and select what they would most likely do next from a number of different scenarios / descriptions

Skill, skills
- An ability or a talent for doing something well

SMART
- **S** is for Specific
- **M** is for Measurable
- **A** is for Achievable
- **R** is for Realistic
- **T** is for Time-based

Social channels, social media
- Your online channels, e.g. LinkedIn, Instagram, Facebook and so on

STAR
- **S**ituation – what were the circumstances? Provide some context for the example
- **T**ask – What did you need to do? Were you given the challenge or was it your idea?
- **A**ction – What did you do? How did you go about it?
- **R**esult – What was the outcome and what did you learn?

Storytelling
- Practical and engaging accounts of events that motivate the audience
- A way of linking different events to illustrate a point of view

Strengths
- Positive behaviours consistently observed throughout different activities

Talent acquisition
- The word talent is wonderfully positive, although the addition of 'acquisition' implies ownership and, in my view, organisations don't *own* their people

Traits
- Often used in conjunction with personality
- Human characteristics consistently displayed

Values
- The things that are important to me
- How I like to live my life
- My attitude to risk
- What I value at work

Video clips   Page 33
  • Short videos up to sixty seconds

Zing (my twist of lime)   Page xiii
  • A combination of who I am, how I work and what I've done
  • Plus, a big dollop of positivity and kindness

> **Top tip** – It's never too late to try something different, although remember to focus on the things that you do well and try not to agonise over what you do less well.

Hello again

At school, I always enjoyed art, social history and gardening. At primary school I was a gardening team leader for two years. Grammar schools in the late sixties weren't really geared up for us creative souls and I didn't want to be an accountant or a teacher.

I was fascinated by what we now call vintage fashion, jumble sales and junk shops, which sparked my interest in designing furniture or clothing. Secretarial training became an attractive early option. A potential gateway to something far more artistic and creative.

My first role as a fully-fledged secretary was in HR in 1972. This set the scene for a successful career, although I didn't always achieve things in the right order. A further dalliance with vintage fashion and a stint as a nanny (a portfolio career before I knew what that meant) made me realise how much I could contribute to managing businesses. In the later seventies, I reimagined myself and returned to HR, determined to carve out a career.

Somehow, working and studying (simultaneously) came naturally to me. After a CIPD post-graduate qualification (1993) came an MSc in HRM & Training (1998). It was a tough gig, although I was rewarded with some great HR challenges and qualifications, as well as opportunities to specialise and to shine.

Then, twenty-one years ago, I embarked on an independent consultancy career, setting up my business in April 2004. My network (an eclectic mix) is important to me and a great source of energy. I'm proud that so many friends, colleagues and clients find pleasure in supporting each other and me.

I've been lucky, as well as successful, and I've so many stories to tell. It didn't seem relevant at the time, but if it helps a few people now, I left school with just three O levels

www.ingramcontent.com/pod-product-compliance
Lightning Source LLC
Chambersburg PA
CBHW052350210326
41597CB00038B/6315